Easy Peasy
Language Arts 4
Parent's Guide

Welcome to the EP Language Arts 4 Parent's Guide!

This little book was created to help you go offline while following EP's Language Arts 4 curriculum. You will need the Language Arts 4 Workbook for your child. Without the online lessons, you will need to be your child's teacher. The directions are here for introducing new topics. The workbook will provide practice and review.

This book also includes objectives for each lesson, materials marked where needed, directions for what to do each lesson, and the complete answer key.

This course covers all language arts topics including: writing, grammar, and spelling. Throughout the year students will be writing creatively and descriptively as well as writing non-fiction as they learn to construct paragraphs and essays. The year ends with a research report.

A little note: To avoid calling all children "he" or the awkward phrasing of "him or her," I've used the plural pronoun when referring to your child, such as, "They need to list ten action verbs and then match them with adverbs. Encourage them to have fun with it. You can brainstorm together if they are slow to get started."

Have a great year.

Lee

Note: We used to call each lesson a day: "Day 1," "Day 2," etc. We've replaced those days with "lessons," but you'll see "day" still in the mini pages in the answer section. Those pages are the same, not outdated, just that one word is changed.

Lesson 1

- Students will: give an oration
- I suggest reading the poem on the Lesson 1 worksheet out loud to your child as they listen. Make it as dramatic and nuanced as you like.
- Discuss any words they don't know and about the meaning and feel of the poem.
- Lesson 1 worksheet
  - They need to practice and then read the poem aloud to an audience. It can be just you. You could record it and share. They need to speak loudly and clearly and not start over. They should just keep going if they stumble.

Lesson 2

- Students will: identify syllables
- Ask your child if they remember what syllables are. A syllable is a chunk of a word; it's how you would break up the word if you were saying it slowly for someone.
- Lesson 2 worksheet
  - Read the directions together. It gives a hint for finding syllables.
  - Ask your child which word on the page had the most syllables.

Lesson 3

- Students will: practice spelling
- Lesson 3 worksheet
  - They are playing hangman today.
  - Here are the words. They are spelling: trouble, deserve, helmet, computer, pencil.

Lesson 4

- Students will: write rhymes
- Together think of words that rhyme with rounded, lighten, darker.
- Lesson 4 worksheet
  - They are to write ten sets of rhyming words. They can use the ideas you just worked on if they need help getting started.

Lesson 5

- Students will: write a poem in the ABAB structure
- They are going to write a poem in the structure of ABAB. That means that the stanza (or section of the poem) will have four lines. The "A" lines rhyme and the "B" lines rhyme. ABAB means that the first line rhymes with the third line, and the second line rhymes with the fourth line.
- Read this example to your child and have them listen for the rhyme pairs.
  - Lend a hand to one another
    In the daily toil of life
    When we meet a weaker brother,

> Let us help him in the strife
> There is none so rich but may
> In his turn, be forced to borrow;
> And the poor man's lot today
> May become our own tomorrow.

- Lesson 5 worksheet
    - They need to write at least four lines to complete the pattern. It's up to them (and you) if they are going to write more.

Lesson 6

- Students will: practice spelling
- Lesson 6 worksheet
    - Give your child the words for the blanks. They are to spell them as best as they can.
        - vacation
        - beach
        - shovel
        - bucket
        - creatures
        - purple
        - swimming
        - ocean
        - floated
    - If they get something wrong, point out which one and try to pronounce it how they wrote it. See if they can fix their own mistake. Make sure they write it out completely the correct way when they have it figured out.

Lesson 7

- Students will: write a limerick
- Lesson 7 worksheet
    - There's an explanation of the poem structure and a sample poem on the page.
    - If it's fun for you (and limericks are fun!) make up some limerick with your child's name.
        - There once was a boy/girl named _____ …
    - They are to make up their own for the page.

Lesson 8

- Students will: practice spelling
- Lesson 8 worksheet
    - They need to find words in the box. You can see the example on the page.
        - If they are stuck, you can give them some words to look for.
            - brains, black, blue, she, quest, queen, amaze, ways, shade, nose, grace, nest.

Lesson 9

- Students will: learn about nouns
- Ask your child what a noun is.
  - They have been learning that a noun is a person, place, or thing. It can also be an idea.
    - Love, hate, and fear are all nouns.
  - Common nouns are regular nouns.
  - Ask your child what a proper noun is.
    - the name of a noun, the name of a person, the name of a place, etc.
  - A concrete noun is something you can see or touch.
  - An abstract noun is something you can't see or touch like love and hope and faith.
  - A compound noun is when two or more words are combined to make a noun.
    - A swimming pool is a compound noun.
    - My father-in-law is a compound noun.
    - Cupcake is a compound noun.
  - A collective noun is when a group is named as a single thing.
    - We say they are, but everyone is. It could be the same people, but we talk about one as plural using are, and one as singular using is. They are. Everyone is.
    - A squad of soldiers is one thing, not many.
    - A school of fish is one thing, not many.
- Lesson 9 worksheet
  - They need to find the nouns and write their own. Make sure they write common, proper, compound, collective, concrete, and abstract nouns.

Lesson 10

- Students will: write a limerick
- Ask your child how many lines are in a limerick and which lines rhyme.
  - 5, AABBA
- Lesson 10 worksheet
  - There is another example of a limerick on their page.

Lesson 11

- Students will: alphabetize words
- Lesson 11 worksheet
  - Here's how they will put the words in alphabetical order.
    - Compare the first letter of each word. Whichever of the letters comes first in the alphabet, that word gets listed first in alphabetical order. Write it on the first line.
    - If the first letter is the same, then you look at the second letter of the words and compare those.
    - If the second letter is the same, then you compare the third letter of each word, etc.

Lesson 12

- Students will: write a limerick
- Ask your child to tell you the structure of a limerick.
  - 5 lines
  - AABBA rhyme
- Lesson 12 worksheet
  - There's another example on the page.

Lesson 13

- Students will: identify common and proper nouns
  - They should be able to do the worksheet without a lesson.

Lesson 14

- Students will: identify action verbs
- Ask your child if they know what an action verb is.
  - An action verb tells what someone or something does.
- Think up a bunch of actions that are happening in your house right now.
  - thinking, talking, sitting
  - Is the fridge humming? Is a notification dinging? Is a dog barking?
- Lesson 14 worksheet
  - They need to identify the action verbs and then write their own.

Lesson 15

- Students will: write an ABAB poem
- Read the poem on the Lesson 15 worksheet page to your child and ask them to listen for the rhyme pattern.
  - It's ABAB.
- Ask your child to look at the poem and figure out the rhythm pattern, how many syllables are in each line.
  - 8,6,8,6
- Lesson 15 worksheet
  - They need to imitate the poem as best they can. Poems don't have to have complete sentences. They can be creative.

Lesson 16

- Students will: practice spelling
- Lesson 16 worksheet
  - Give your child the words for the blanks. They are to spell them as best as they can.
    - called
    - exciting

- horses
- twenty
- million
- Saturday
- longest

  o If they get something wrong, point out which one and try to pronounce it how they wrote it. See if they can fix their own mistake. Make sure they write it out completely the correct way when they have it figured out.

Lesson 17

- Students will: write a poem
- Lesson 17 worksheet
  o The goal is to write two stanzas. Each stanza could be two lines. They don't have to rhyme, but it's fun to make them rhyme.
  o If your child is stressing over this and giving up before they begin, come up with some little poems for inspiration.
    - The color blue
      is so true.
      The color red
      makes me want to go to bed.
  o The most important part is to believe they can do it and try. Some will embrace it; some will just get through. Either is okay, but they all need to get it done. Don't let them skip it!

Lesson 18

- Students will: practice spelling
- Lesson 18 worksheet
  o They are to unscramble the words. There are definitions to help them.
  o If your child is stuck, they can turn back through their workbook. These are words they've spelled before, except maybe the first, vocabulary.

Lesson 19

- Students will: identify action and linking verbs
- Ask your child what an action verb is.
  o It tells what someone or something does.
- A linking verb tells that something exists. Here are some of the linking verbs.
  o am, is, are, was, were, will, be, has been, had been, have been, become, became
  o You can memorize this list by singing it to any tune. Try "Twinkle, Twinkle Little Star" if you can't think of your own tune.
- It's a linking verb if you can replace "it" with an equals sign. Tara is happy. Tara = happy. You can't write Tara loves her dog and Tara = her dog.
  o There are a few tricky verbs that can be linking verbs or action verbs. I feel sick can be I = sick and be a linking verb, but it could also be I feel the soft fur on the

kitten, and it would be an action verb because you aren't equal to the kitten's soft fur.

- Lesson 19 worksheet
  - They just need to identify what the verb is and what type of verb. Some verbs can be two words, like "will be" and "has been."

Lesson 20

- Students will: write a poem
- Lesson 20 worksheet
  - There's an example I wrote on their page for an idea if they are stuck getting started.
  - They could use the same idea and pick a different time of day, for instance, as a way to get started, but again, that's just if they are stuck. Repetition is a tool used by poets, though.

Lesson 21

- Students will: practice spelling
- Lesson 21 worksheet
  - Make sure to pronounce all of these words with the OO sound.
    - scoop
    - routine
    - wound
    - loop
    - hoop
    - souvenir
    - mood
    - raccoon
    - troop
    - food
    - booth
    - broom
  - If they get something wrong, point out which one and try to pronounce it how they wrote it. See if they can fix their own mistake. Make sure they write it out completely the correct way when they have it figured out.

Lesson 22

- Students will: write a story
- Lesson 22 worksheet
  - The writing prompt is to write about your first day stranded on an island. You could talk about this before they begin. Most kids are great at coming up with stories when they aren't writing, so get the story started just by talking. Who is there? What are they going to eat? Are they going to try to build a boat to escape or build a home to live there?

Lesson 23

- Students will: practice spelling
- Lesson 23 worksheet
  - They should use the sentences and pictures to write the words in the blanks. If they are stuck, you can remind them that they all have the OO sound. Wait until they have filled in all that they can before you help. If they are stuck on any, you can let them know they can turn back to Lesson 21 to see the possible words.

Lesson 24

- Students will: write common and proper nouns, action and linking verbs
- Lesson 24 worksheet
  - They need to write five of each. Encourage them to be creative and use a variety. For nouns they should use people, places, things, and ideas. Don't let them skip including an abstract noun.

Lesson 25

- Students will: write directions
- Lesson 25 worksheet
  - The writing prompt is about writing steps to follow to complete some survival skill, such as building a shelter. (These prompts come from Level 4 because they are reading *Swiss Family Robinson*.) If your child doesn't like the prompt, they can write the steps for anything.
  - The important things are to start with an introduction sentence and to write out detailed directions with numbered steps.

Lesson 26

- Students will: write each of the four types of sentences
- Lesson 26 worksheet
  - Read through the words, definitions, and examples together.

Lesson 27

- Students will: write each of the four types of sentences
- Lesson 27 worksheet
  - Look at the directions and ask your child to tell you what type each sentence is. You can refer to Lesson 26 if you aren't sure on one.
  - They can just list sentences, but let them know they can get a high five and/or hug if they turn them into a story.

Lesson 28

- Students will: write each of the four types of sentences
- Lesson 28 worksheet
  - Look at the directions and ask your child again to tell you what type each sentence is. You can refer to Lesson 26 if you aren't sure on one.
  - They can just list sentences, or they can try to turn them all into a story. Give them a high five and/or hug if they make a story.

Lesson 29

- Students will: identify common and proper nouns
- Lesson 29 worksheet
  - They need to write the words to categorize them. In the second part they will match them up.
  - See if your child can figure out why it might be better to use a proper noun instead of a common noun in their writing.
    - A proper noun makes their writing more specific. It's a German shepherd, not just a dog. It's Save – a – Lot, not just a grocery store. More specific writing gives the reader a better picture of the story which makes your story more interesting to read.

Lesson 30

- Students will: write a story using each of the four types of sentences
- Lesson 30 worksheet
  - The writing prompt is to write about being alone. They can write their own idea if they have one.
  - The requirement is to use each type of sentence.

Lesson 31 (book)

- Students will: practice their handwriting, identify common and proper nouns as well as linking and action verbs
- Lesson 31 worksheet
  - They need to copy a <u>long</u> sentence from somewhere. Feel free to make them do it again if they forget punctuation, capitalization, or it's illegible.
  - There's a little grammar review at the bottom of the page.

Lesson 32 (book)

- Students will: write each of the four types of sentences
- Lesson 32 worksheet
  - They need to use a book, or whatever written material you have around you, to find each type of sentence and copy it.
  - They need to make sure to copy carefully all the punctuation and capitalization.

Lesson 33

- Students will: identify the main idea of a paragraph
- Ask your child what the main idea is of this paragraph.
  - I love going to the park. I love all the green trees and grass. I love going on walks along the paths. I would go to the park every day if I could.
    - The main idea is that the author loves going to the park. Often the main idea of a paragraph is found in the first sentence or the first couple of sentences. Sometimes the main idea isn't specifically told to you.
    - The rest of the sentences are called the details. They tell you more about the main idea.
- Lesson 33 worksheet
  - They have to pick the main idea out from the three sentences given. One is the main idea. The others tell more about it.

Lesson 34

- Students will: identify the main idea of paragraphs
- Lesson 34 worksheet
  - They should be able to do this on their own. The main idea isn't always directly written in the beginning of the paragraphs. They will have to infer what the main point of the paragraph is, but they are given options.

Lesson 35

- Students will: write a creative story
- Lesson 35 worksheet
  - This is a continuation of our life stranded on an island. They can write their own story, or if they liked their all alone story and it had a different setting, they could continue with that story by finding something in that setting.

Lesson 36 (copy)

- Students will: practice handwriting, identify the main idea
- Lesson 36 worksheet
  - They need to copy a sentence. Encourage them to find a good sentence, something descriptive, funny, exciting, something worth copying.
    - Make sure to hold them to some standard for their copywork.
  - There are main idea paragraphs at the bottom of the page.

Lesson 37

- Students will: write a creative story
- Lesson 37 worksheet
  - They can use the writing prompt about finding a message in a bottle or write their own creative story. The point is to write. This isn't the time to correct a lot of

spelling or punctuation. You can point it out if they didn't capitalize the first letter in each sentence, but don't mark up their page. Let them enjoy the creative process.

- o If they like their story, they could type it up and make it correct.
- o You could save this for their portfolio.

Lesson 38

- • Students will: practice spelling
- • Lesson 38 worksheet
  - o This a word search. The words are on their page. These words they've seen in other spelling exercises.

Lesson 39

- • Students will: demonstrate reading comprehension
- • Lesson 39 worksheet
  - o They will read the story and answer the questions.

Lesson 40

- • Students will: write a dialogue
- • Lesson 40 worksheet
  - o Take a look at the directions on the page and the example quotation.
  - o Everything said goes in quotes.
  - o Every time the speaker changes, they have to start writing on a new line.
  - o If they are stuck, have a conversation and let them record it for their dialogue.

Lesson 41(book)

- • Students will: practice handwriting (also imitate grammar, style, etc.)
- • Lesson 41 worksheet
  - o They need a sentence to copy. Ideally, they would choose a sentence from quality literature.
  - o Require it to be correctly and neatly copied.
  - o They are to come up with verbs at the bottom of the page. Encourage your child to be creative with it and praise them when they are!

Lesson 42

- • Students will: write a dialogue
- • Lesson 42 worksheet
  - o Read the writing prompt on the page and talk about it. What would they ask for first if they had been stranded and alone for a long time? What would they want to know about from back home?

- o Their page reminds them to write neatly and carefully, but this isn't a handwriting practice. I want you to remind them that whatever is being spoken needs to go in quotation marks and that they need to start a new line whenever the speaker changes.

Lesson 43

- • Students will: practice spelling
- • Lesson 43 worksheet
    - o Give them these words to spell. Point out any words that are wrong and let them try again. If they are stuck, give them the sound for the part of the word that's wrong. Encourage them to think through what it should be. Then have them rewrite the word correctly right there on the page.
        - ▪ remember
        - ▪ neutral
        - ▪ happened
        - ▪ product
        - ▪ retain
        - ▪ council
        - ▪ mortal
        - ▪ measure
        - ▪ early
        - ▪ utensil
        - ▪ canopy
        - ▪ abundant

Lesson 44

- • Students will: punctuate dialogue
- • Let's look at how you punctuate dialogue.
    - o The quotation marks go around what is being said. "I'm telling you to come here."
    - o Punctuation always comes <u>before</u> the quotation marks. That's true whether it's a comma, a period, an exclamation point, or a question mark. The punctuation comes before the quotation mark.
    - o Here's the tricky part. "Come here," I said. Even though "come here" is a sentence, I didn't put a period there. I used a comma. If you were to tell someone about this, you would say, "She said come here." You would say it all as one sentence, right? The "I said" part is part of the sentence, it tells us about what's being said.
    - o Review the examples on the page together:
        - ▪ "Let's have dinner this weekend."
            - • Point out: end punctuation before quotation marks
        - ▪ "Let's have dinner this weekend," he said to her.
            - • Point out: comma instead of period and inside quotation marks, lowercase "he"

- He said, "Let's have dinner."
  - Point out: comma after said and before quotation marks, uppercase "Let's" as it's beginning a sentence, even though it's within a sentence
- Lesson 44 worksheet
  - They are going to add the punctuation and underline what needs to be capitalized.
  - Correct this worksheet right away.
    - Tell them which ones are wrong and ask them to see if they can figure out what's wrong. If they can't find it, give them a hint, by letting them know if it's punctuation or capitalization. Try to keep from just telling them or marking what's wrong.
  - Have them go back to their dialogue on Lesson 42 and correct the punctuation.

Lesson 45

- Students will: write a comic strip dialogue
- Lesson 45 worksheet
  - They are to create a comic strip. This is just another way to write dialogue. They will draw the characters, the action, and write what they are saying at the top of the box in quotes. They can add sound effects without quotes. Thud!

Lesson 46

- Students will: begin research
- Lesson 46 worksheet
  - They need to pick a person that they are interested in, or you can help them pick someone from history that you want them to know about. They could pair this up with what they are learning in history right now.
  - They are going to research this person and write an essay about them.
  - Today they need to pick the person and gather five facts about the person.
  - They need to write one fact per line.

Lesson 47

- Students will: research
- Lesson 47 worksheet
  - They need to gather five more facts. They need to write one fact per line so that they can be organized.

Lesson 48

- Students will: organize their facts to prepare for an essay
- Lesson 48 worksheet
  - They need to divide up their ten facts into the three categories on the page. These will become the three body paragraphs of their essay.
  - In the boxes they just need to write the fact numbers.

- If a box only has one or two, have your child look for more facts for that category. There's a spot on the page for extra facts.
- They should have at least three for each category.

Lesson 49

- Students will: punctuate a dialogue
- They will be adding in dialogue punctuation and correcting capitalization.
- Lesson 49 worksheet
  - I think it would be easiest to go to the page and look at the first one together. These are longer than they had before.
    - Have your child read the sentence and tell you what's being said. They need to put quotes around it.
    - Then they need to identify the two sentences.
      - Every sentence needs to begin with a capital letter and end with punctuation. They should put those in.
    - "Where have you been, Mom?" asked Jeffrey. "We've been looking all over for you!" (or a period instead of an exclamation point)

Lesson 50

- Students will: write a story with dialogue
- Lesson 50 worksheet
  - They are to write a story. It can be mostly dialogue. It must contain some dialogue. They should pay attention to dialogue punctuation and start a new line every time the speaker changes.
  - If they are stuck, have them imagine their best friend just came over. What would they say to them?

Lesson 51

- Students will: organize a paragraph for the body of their essay
- Lesson 51 worksheet
  - They are to take their who/what facts and put them together on this page.
  - They need to choose their three best facts. They can add a fourth if they are all deemed important by your child.
  - They will also introduce the facts with a main idea sentence. All of their facts should be details that tell about this main idea.
  - They will also give a concluding statement. This restates the main idea in a new way. It can answer the question, "So what?"
    - What was the big deal? Why did you just tell them that information? What makes it important?
  - Here's an example.
    - main idea: George Washington was a leader in many ways.
    - detail #1: He was general of the troops in America during the American Revolution.

- detail #2: He led Congress' delegates in forming the Constitution.
- detail #3: He became the first president to serve America under the Constitution.
- closing sentence: He was successful no matter what hat he was wearing.

Lesson 52 (book, Note: This might best be completed during their reading time for today.)

- Students will: identify transitions in writing
- Lesson 52 worksheet
  - Their worksheet gives a few examples of transitions.
  - Have your child read or look through a book and find three sentences that use transitions. They are to copy them onto their page, as well as come up with some ideas for transitions.
  - I point out transitions to my kids when we watch movies. They will have the same word repeated in the end of one scene and then in the start of the next scene, or it will mention something at the end of one scene and then show it in the opening of the next scene.

Lesson 53

- Students will: organize their where/when paragraph
- Lesson 53 worksheet
  - These sentences are going to be put together into paragraphs. They need an intro and details that tell about that main idea, and they need a "So what?" conclusion.
  - Here's the continuing example.
    - Whenever and wherever his country asked him to be, that's where Washington could be found. He was born in Mount Vernon, Virginia. He returned there to live after serving as general during the Revolution from 1775 until 1781. He wanted to retire then and there, but he moved to Philadelphia to live when he was unanimously voted president of the United States. He was a true example of what a politician is meant to be, a servant of the people.

Lesson 54 (scissors)

- Students will: practice creating dialogue
- Lesson 54 worksheet
  - They are to cut out the words and punctuation and create one or more dialogues with them.

Lesson 55

- Students will: organize their why/how paragraph
- Lesson 55 worksheet
  - Fill in the hamburger for today.

- o Washington was a natural leader because he was a man people respected and trusted. There is a famous story about Washington cutting down his father's cherry tree. When questioned, Washington confesses saying, "I cannot tell a lie." While this story may be make believe, it shows what people believed about Washington. People, including his troops and members of Congress, found him completely trustworthy, making it easy to respect him. This ability to win people's trust and respect made him a great leader.

Lesson 56

- Students will: write an introductory paragraph, identify proper nouns
- This paragraph takes a different structure than the body paragraphs they've been working on.
  - o It should start with a sentence that makes people curious or that catches their attention.
    - Some ideas are to start with a question, a quotation, a joke or funny story, or a surprising statement.
  - o The final sentence of the introductory paragraph will be the main idea for the whole essay. They should think about what is in their hamburgers and what the main idea of it all should be.
  - o Here's an example of an introductory paragraph.
    - opening sentence: Ever wonder what makes someone great?
    - middle (no details yet): History has many greats. One man in particular was a great leader at an important time in America's history.
    - main idea of the whole biography (called the thesis): George Washington was a great leader when America needed one.
  - o Other opening sentences could be:
    - George Washington wasn't the first president in America. (surprising fact)
      - There were other presidents that came before him, but he was the first to hold office after the Constitution officially created the position over the American people. President was the only title George Washington held…
    - George Washington said, "I hope I shall possess firmness and virtue enough to maintain what I consider the most enviable of all titles, the character of an honest man." (quotation)
      - George Washington held many titles that others would consider enviable, but his character, which held honesty as more important than title, is what made him a great…
- Lesson 56 worksheet
  - o They are to write their introductory paragraph.
  - o There's a quick and easy activity at the bottom of the page.

Lesson 57

- Students will: write using onomatopoeia
- Today they are going to write using onomatopoeia (on-uh-mat-uh-pee-uh).
- Together think of words that make the sound they describe. For me the easiest way to think about it is that they are the words you would say in a fun way when reading a children's book out loud.
  - buzz, crash, bang, burp, moo,...
  - There are examples on their workbook page as well, but think of as many as you can before you look at it.
- Lesson 57 worksheet
  - The directions are to describe their day yesterday. They can describe an imaginary day if they like. The important thing is to use a sound word, onomatopoeia, in each sentence.
  - Have them read it to you (or to the whole family) when they are done and to read it in a fun way.

Lesson 58

- Students will: write a conclusion paragraph, identify linking verbs
- The first sentence of their conclusion should restate the main idea in a different way. The final sentence should try to answer the question, "So what?" You could use the word "I" in the last sentence. Why was this important to you?
- Here's my George Washington example.
  - main idea (in different words, not the same exact sentence)
    - George Washington was a great leader when America was struggling to be independent and to stand on its own.
  - middle (no new details)
    - He united his troops as general and the country as president by commanding their respect.
  - closing sentence
    - I think God put George Washington in the right place at the right time, just who America needed in order to become the United States of America.
- Lesson 58 worksheet
  - They are going to write their conclusion. There's also a little linking verb activity on the page.

Lesson 59

- Students will: identify pronouns, correct verb forms, and meanings of idiomatic expressions
- Lesson 59 worksheet
  - This has three short activities.

Lesson 60

- Students will: write a letter
- Here's the format of a letter.
    - A letter begins with a salutation, something like, Dear Mom. That begins with a capital letter and is followed by a comma.
    - That is followed by the body of the letter which starts on a new line.
    - The letter is closed on a new line with a word like sincerely, respectively, yours truly, or just love. That is also followed by a comma and begins with a capital letter!
    - Lastly, you sign or write your name.
- Lesson 60 worksheet
    - They are told to write their mom a letter as someone from the time period they are studying. They can write any letter. I was just trying to spice it up and make it interesting.
        - However, if they do happen to be studying ancient Egypt and want to write in hieroglyphics, please allow it, but they still need to show capital letters and put in commas where appropriate. It should look like a letter. This practice is about the form, not the writing.

Lesson 61

- Students will: add transitions and edit their five paragraph essay
- They are going to take the five paragraphs they have prepared and turn them into an essay over three days. They could type this if that's preferable to them instead of writing this out in their workbook.
    - They are mostly copying, but they should think about adding transition words to the beginnings of their paragraphs.
        - Transition words include: as a result, on the other hand, however, …or just first, second, finally
        - A good way to transition is to mention the previous paragraph. Here's an example of the first sentence of the paragraph about George Washington as president after talking about him as general.
            - While he was a great leader during times of war, he was also a great leader in times of peace.
- Lesson 61 worksheet
    - Each paragraph should start on a new line and be indented. They should add a transition to the beginning of their who/what paragraph.
    - They should read it out loud and change anything that makes them stumble or that just didn't sound right.

Lesson 62

- Students will: work on their five paragraph essay
- Lesson 62 worksheet
  - They are going to write the when/where and why/how paragraphs today.
  - They each need a transition.
  - When they are done, they should read it out loud and change anything that makes them stumble.

Lesson 63

- Students will: work on editing their five paragraph essay
- Lesson 63 worksheet
  - They will copy down their paragraph.
  - Now to editing, they should make sure they have long and short sentences. If they don't have any commas, they should make some compound sentences.
    - Can they include a sentence with and, with but, with an exclamation point, with a question mark?
    - The more varied the sentences are, the more interesting the biography will be.

Lesson 64

- Students will: finish their five paragraph essay
- Today they should check for capitalization, punctuation, and spelling.
- They should also choose one verb and look it up in a thesaurus and choose a better word.
  - They can also look for any common nouns that should be replaced with proper nouns to make it more specific and interesting.
- Reading the whole thing out loud to check it would be a good idea.
  - My book *The King Will Make a Way* was written in one month and edited over six months. Tell that to your kids, so they understand the importance of putting time into editing.
- They should finalize their essay. If they typed it, they could print a final draft. This is something to save, even if it's not pretty.
- Lesson 64 worksheet
  - This has a page for feedback from three audience members.
  - Have your child read their essay in front of the family or just pass it around to be read.

Lesson 65

- Students will: write a descriptive paragraph
- Lesson 65 worksheet
  - If they don't have a picture in mind from a book, they can just look out the window or around the room they are in.

o If they include what they see, hear, and smell, as well as the variety of sentence types mentioned on the page, then give them a high five and/or hug.

Lesson 66

- Students will: write an introduction and conclusion to their descriptive paragraph, write descriptive words
- On Lesson 65 they wrote a description. They need to think of a creative way to get a reader interested in reading their description. Can they make the reader curious? This will become their introduction sentence.
    o This is going to become the first sentence of the paragraph they wrote on Lesson 65.
- Then they need to write a conclusion sentence.
    o It should wrap up the story, give a thought, a feeling, a connection.
    o Together think about how movies give you a warm, fuzzy feeling at the end. That's their conclusion.
    o A conclusion should give them something to feel or to think about.
- Lesson 66 worksheet
    o They will write their introduction and conclusion sentences.
    o Then there are words for them to rewrite. There are examples on the page about how to be more specific in their descriptions.

Lesson 67

- Students will: write a book summary
- They should read their whole descriptive paragraph out loud and edit it.
- They need to pick a book they've recently read or know really well for their next writing assignment.
- Ask your child about the main character(s), who the book was about, the setting, where it took place, and the plot, the main idea of the book.
- Lesson 67 worksheet
    o They need to put that into three to five sentences which summarize the book.

Lesson 68

- Students will: continue writing a book summary
- Ask your child what the best part of the book was. It could be part of the story they liked or how funny the author is.
- Lesson 68 worksheet
    o They need to write a paragraph. The first sentence should be the main idea that this is the best part of the book. Then they should write a total of three to five sentences describing that part of the book. Their conclusion sentence could say why it was the best part.

Lesson 69

- Students will: continue writing a book summary
- Ask your child what was the worst thing about the book. It doesn't have to be something from the plot. It could be about the writing.
- Lesson 69 worksheet
  - They need to write three to five sentences again, another paragraph.
    - It should have an intro, details, and conclusion. If they need more to say, they can quote the book.

Lesson 70

- Students will: write an introduction to a book report
- They have been writing this all week. Now they need their introduction and conclusion paragraphs.
- Lesson 70 worksheet
  - They just need to write their introduction today. There are directions on the page. The title of the book needs to have all the main words capitalized and it needs to be underlined (or italicized but that's hard with handwriting).
    - The last sentence should be the main idea, what they thought about the book.

Lesson 71

- Students will: write a concluding paragraph to a book report
- Today they are writing their conclusion. Ask your child what conclusions are supposed to do.
  - leave them with a feeling or something to think about
- Lesson 71 worksheet
  - They have directions on their page.

Lesson 72

- Students will: edit a book report
- Lesson 72 worksheet
  - They should apply the checklist to editing their book report.
- Have your child read their book report out loud to help with editing.
  - How can they add transitions between the paragraphs? What needs changing?
  - Can two sentences be combined with a comma and conjunction (and, but, or...)?
  - Can two thoughts be combined into a longer sentence using because, if, however, unless, since...?
  - Change a verb to make it more exciting

Lesson 73

- Students will: present a book report
- Have your child read their book report out loud to look for problems.
  - Reading it out loud is a great technique to use. It helps you read each word instead of skimming as we tend to do when we read.
  - It also helps you spot areas that might trip up a reader who wasn't familiar with it.
- Have your child read their book report to you or an audience, or just share it to be read. This is something you might want to hang on to for a portfolio.
- Lesson 73 worksheet
  - There is a page for feedback from the audience.

Lesson 74

- Students will: identify adjectives
- Have your child identify the adjective in this sentence. They have two cars.
  - Two is the adjective. It is describing cars.
- Lesson 74 worksheet
  - They just need to find and underline the adjectives.

Lesson 75

- Students will: write a formal letter
- There is an example on their worksheet.
  - It starts with their address, then the date, then the person and address it's going to.
  - That's followed by the greeting, the salutation.
  - That's followed by the body, the message.
  - It ends with their closing, name and title.
  - The greeting and closing both begin with a capital letter and are followed by a comma.
- Lesson 75 worksheet
  - Write a letter to the president. You can decide if you want to mail it or not.

Lesson 76

- Students will: identify adjectives
- Lesson 76 worksheet
  - They need to mark the fish with adjectives.

Lesson 77

- Students will: write creatively
- Lesson 77 worksheet
  - They are to write a fun story, a story that makes them smile and laugh as they write it.

Lesson 78

- Students will: edit
- Lesson 78 worksheet
  - First they can brainstorm creative adjectives and then creatively combine the sentences on the bottom part of the page. They can change the sentences a little.
    - Examples:
      - I like pizza with cheese and pepperoni, but maybe you like those things too.
      - It was cold outside when we went to the lake, but we swam anyway, and it was a fun day.
- Then they need to add adjectives to their story from Lesson 77 and combine sentences to make some longer ones. There shouldn't be three in a row of the same type of sentence (such as three simple short sentences). Note: The exception would be if they were actually doing it for its literary effect.

Lesson 79

- Students will: identify adjectives, edit
- They should read their story out loud and correct anything that stands out to them.
- Ask your child what the adjective is in this sentence, "This is the book."
  - It's *the* book; it is telling you which book.
    - The is the adjective.
  - The, A, and An are called articles and most people consider that a separate part of speech from adjective, so they aren't always included in adjective lists, but they are used like adjectives.
  - Other words that are always adjectives are possessives like your, my, and their. Again, these have their own part of speech, but they are used like adjectives in describing nouns.
    - It's their house. It's my book. It's your job.
    - They describe the noun.
- Lesson 79 worksheet
  - They need to identify all the adjectives. They should go ahead and find articles and possessives as adjectives.
  - They are looking for words that describe a noun.

Lesson 80

- Students will: present their story
- Your child needs to make sure their story is ready to present.
- Then they should read it out loud for an audience (maybe just you). They should be loud and clear and expressive and try to make you laugh.
- Lesson 80 worksheet
  - There are places for feedback from three people.

Lesson 81

- Students will: create a character
- Lesson 81 worksheet
  - They are going to create a main character for another story.
  - They need to name their character and give him or her an age. It doesn't have to be a person, but it has to have a personality.
  - The more your child knows about this character the better the story will be.
  - They aren't writing their story on these days, just making lists of ideas.

Lesson 82

- Students will: create a setting and a plot
- Lesson 82 worksheet
  - They need to decide where their character is and what he or she is doing.
  - A great story has a hero in trouble. Does the main character have a problem?

Lesson 83

- Students will: create a plot
- Lesson 83 worksheet
  - They need to decide what happens in the middle and end of the story.
  - This is usually the hero, the main character, trying to solve their problem and things going wrong and then finally being able to solve their problem.
  - They aren't writing the story as much as planning the story.

Lesson 84 (blue, green, red – crayons or colored pencils)

- Students will: identify nouns, verbs, adjectives
- Lesson 84 worksheet
  - If you don't have colors, they can make their own shading/marking techniques to label the parts of speech.

Lesson 85

- Students will: write a fiction story
- Lesson 85 worksheet
  - They will use their pages from Lessons 81-83 to start writing their story. They have today and Lesson 86 to write their first draft.

Lesson 86

- Students will: finish writing a fiction story
- Lesson 86 worksheet
  - They should finish writing their story today.

Lesson 87

- Students will: edit their story
- Your child should read their story out loud and edit it. If a sentence goes on too long, they should consider a comma and conjunction. Can they make it better with adjectives?
- They should read the story to you and see if you laugh.
- Lesson 87 worksheet
  - There is a page for their audience to give their feedback.

Lesson 88

- Students will: practice spelling
- Lesson 88 worksheet
  - Here are the words for the page.
    - building
    - revise
    - carefully
    - scientists
    - inside
    - leisure
    - seizure
    - rupture
    - pleasure
    - vulture
    - culture
    - measure
  - If they get something wrong, point out which one and maybe pronounce it how they wrote it. See if they can fix their own mistake. Make sure they write it out completely the correct way when they have it figured out.

Lesson 89

- Students will: practice parts of speech, punctuation, capitalization, descriptive writing
- Lesson 89 worksheet
  - There is a sentence to copy on the page. They need to follow the directions carefully.
  - There are two other short activities.

Lesson 90

- Students will: write a story
- Lesson 90 worksheet
  - This is a one-day assignment.
  - If your child is stuck getting started, dream up together a mysterious person you saw walking down the street and make up where they came from and what they were doing.
    - Then they just need to write it down.

Lesson 91

- Students will: write
- Lesson 91 worksheet
  - Read the quote on the page and talk about the feeling of delicious. Help them think about how they feel on the inside when they take a bite of something SOOOO good.
  - What else gives them a good feeling like that?
  - They just need to tell about it. It can just be one great sentence.

Lesson 92

- Students will: write a description
- They are going to need to describe a person. You could start by thinking of a favorite character in a book or movie or TV show. What can your child describe about that person?
  - Their description shouldn't just be what they look like, but how they act, what they are like in their thinking and behavior.
- Lesson 92 worksheet
  - They are told to describe a sibling or a parent. You can let them describe someone else, but it might be enlightening to ask them to describe you!

Lesson 93

- Students will: identify the correct meaning of homophones
- Lesson 93 worksheet
  - They need to match the words and their definitions. Each word has another that sounds like it but is spelled differently, a homophone.

Lesson 94

- Students will: write a descriptive sentence
- Lesson 94 worksheet
  - Look at the page together. Read the sentence and then skip to the next directions on the page before they copy it. Go back to the sentence and have your child point

out how the sentence shows what she did, how she did it, how she felt, and what it looked like.
- o Then they can copy the sentence and write their own with the same level of description.

Lesson 95

- Students will: write a story with homophones
- Lesson 95 worksheet
  - o They can look back at Lesson 93's page for ideas.
  - o Hint: Easy homophones are their, there, and they're.
  - o Give a high five and/or hug for using more than two homophones.

Lesson 96

- Students will: practice spelling
- Lesson 96 worksheet
  - o They are to find words in the puzzle. There aren't certain ones they are supposed to find.
  - o If they are stuck here are some to look for: donut, taken, cards, yards, vine, rise, bake, none, swag, pale.

Lesson 97

- Students will: practice spelling
- Lesson 97 worksheet
  - o Have your child write these words.
    - government
    - pledge
    - equation
    - average
    - cartridge
    - knowledge
    - public
    - private
    - academic
    - athlete
    - seventy
    - forty
  - o If they get something wrong, point out which one and try to pronounce it how they wrote it. See if they can fix their own mistake. Make sure they write it out completely the correct way when they have it figured out.

Lesson 98

- Students will: identify types of nouns
- See if your child remembers these types of nouns: common, proper, abstract, collective, compound.
  - regular, names, can't see and touch, all-as-one like team or traffic, two together like cupcake or ice rink

- Lesson 98 worksheet
  - This is multiple choice.

Lesson 99

- Students will: identify idiom meanings
- Lesson 99 worksheet
  - This is also multiple choice. If they ask about one of them, instead of giving the answer, try to think of a time you would use it and give an example of its use.

Lesson 100

- Students will: practice spelling
- Lesson 100 worksheet
  - They are to fill in the letters to make words. They should probably use a pencil with an eraser!

Lesson 101

- Students will: be introduced to adverbs
- Today they are seeing adverbs for the first time. They describe verbs, adjectives or other adverbs.
  - If you quickly go somewhere, quickly is telling how you went. Quickly is the adverb.
  - We often go on walks. Often tells how you go. Often is the adverb.
  - It's really dark. Really tells about how dark it is.
  - In the example sentence on their page, the adverbs are rather slowly. Slowly tells how the car is going and rather describes how slowly it is going.
  - They are all adverbs.
    - Often, but not always, adverbs end in the letters LY.
    - Adverbs tell us how.
- Lesson 101 worksheet
  - Read together the sentence on the page and talk about the mood in the story at that point.
    - The heavy fog, the fact that it's dark even though it is day, and the slow driving produce a sad kind of mood.

Lesson 102

- Students will: write expressive sentences, identify parts of speech
- Lesson 102 worksheet
  - Read the sentence at the top of the page.
  - Ask your child what the children in the room might be thinking based on what the sentence tells us about what they looked like.
  - There are two sentences they are to write. Ask your child what someone acts like when they are happy or scared. They need to describe those things instead of saying they were happy or scared.

Lesson 103

- Students will: write a sentence with dependent clauses
- Lesson 103 worksheet
  - Read the sentence together. See if your child can find three adverbs (two are the same word). They each describe adjectives.
    - very soon, very hard, rather dull
  - Go through the directions before they begin. They are going to imitate the structure of the sentence by adding clauses, groups of words.
    - They need to be careful to use the commas where shown. These are all dependent clauses. That means they are unnecessary words. The sentence can exist without them and do just fine. However, to write great descriptive sentences, you need to use extra words!

Lesson 104

- Students will: write a long sentence
- Ask your child what an adverb is. It describes a verb or adjective or other adverb.
- Lesson 104 worksheet
  - There is a sample sentence on the page. They are to write a long sentence with six adjectives and two verbs, at least.
  - Give your child a high five and/or hug for including an adverb.

Lesson 105

- Students will: write a long sentence, write a creative story
- Lesson 105 worksheet
  - There's a sentence on the page to read and imitate.
    - Here's my example following the directions.
      - The thing I'm most proud of is my ability to stay calm in an emergency.
      - The thing I'm most proud of, besides my charm and unfading beauty, is my ability to stay calm in an emergency.

Lesson 106

- Students will: learn about different types of adjectives and use adjectives in their writing
- Ask your child what an adjective is and to give an example of how an adjective can be used to describe a noun.
    - describe a noun, furry dog
- How can an adjective be used to describe a pronoun?
    - He is funny.
- Which word is the adjective in this next sentence? I want more ice cream.
    - More describes ice cream.
- Which word is the adjective in this next sentence? I want this ice cream.
    - This describes ice cream.
- Interrogative adjectives ask a question. Which shoes? These shoes.
    - Which and these are adjectives; both are used to talk about shoes.
- Comparative and superlative adjectives say something is more or most.
    - He is tall. She is taller. He is tallest.
    - This is good. That is better. Those are best.
    - What are the comparative and superlative adjectives for bad?
        - bad, worse, worst
- We've already talked about how articles and possessives are always a type of adjective.
    - the bike, my bike, an alligator, your alligator
- Lesson 106 worksheet
    - They need to identify the parts of speech and write about themselves with adjectives.

Lesson 107

- Students will: write adverbs, practice spelling
- Lesson 107 worksheet
    - They are to write adverbs to describe how they could do their work and how they could treat their family. You can come up with some ideas together if they are slow to get started.
        - They could do their work accurately, diligently, crazily…
        - They could treat their family rudely or respectfully.

Lesson 108

- Students will: identify adverbs, grammar review, begin work on an autobiography
- Give your child this reminder about adverbs.
    - Adverbs describe how something is done. How did you walk? Quickly. How did you cook? Skillfully. How did you eat? Sloppily.
    - Read the following paragraph and have your child listen for the two LY adverbs.
        - The first night she spent in her attic was a thing Sara never forgot. During its passing she lived through a wild, unchildlike woe of which she never spoke to anyone about her. There was no one who would have understood. It was, indeed, well for her that as she lay awake in the darkness her mind

was forcibly distracted, now and then, by the strangeness of her surroundings. It was, perhaps, well for her that she was reminded by her small body of material things. If this had not been so, the anguish of her young mind might have been too great for a child to bear. But while the night was passing she scarcely knew that she had a body at all or remembered any other thing than one.

- forcibly and scarcely
- forcibly distracted, scarcely knew

- Lesson 108 worksheet
  - They are to correct the mistakes as review of punctuation and capitalization.
  - There are three autobiography pages in the back of the book. They are labeled with Lesson 108. They are there so that they can be used all together as a book. You can think about printing out pictures to include where there are spaces for pictures. They are going to fill out the information about themselves and about their parents. They should do this neatly to be something to keep.

Lesson 109

- Students will: distinguish between when to use good vs. well
- Good is an adjective and well is an adverb. You work well, but you do a good job.
  - Well is describing how you work and good is describing the job you did.
- Why does this sentence use good and not well?
  - The fried chicken tasted so good.
    - How did it taste? Good!
    - We're not describing how well he did at tasting the fried chicken; we're talking about the taste of the chicken.
- Lesson 109 worksheet
  - They just need to put in well or good.

Lesson 110

- Students will: write a fictional story
- Lesson 110 worksheet
  - They are going to produce a work of fiction. It is to be about them and set in their normal life, but it's going to be completely untrue.

Lesson 111

- Students will: write a sentence using however, write a sentence using adverbs, work on their autobiography
- Here are some examples of adverbs: usually, normally, often, occasionally, yesterday, upstairs, soon, today, yet, definitely, probably, obviously, rarely, never, sometimes, only, also, last
- Lesson 111 worksheet
  - There is a sentence and example on the page to imitate.

- o Then they are to write a sentence with adverbs. Reward them if they use more than two.
- o There are two sibling pages to complete in the back of the book as part of the autobiography. They are labeled as Lesson 111.
  - ▪ You can print out the number of pages you need to complete that section and staple them in. The site has the sibling pages on Lesson 111 on the Language Arts 4 page.

Lesson 112

- Students will: collect information for their autobiography, practice spelling, write a sentence beginning with a dependent clause
- Lesson 112 worksheet
  - o They just need to follow the directions on the page.
  - o There are four pages on their grandparents to fill out in the back of the book. They need to pay attention to if it says paternal (their father's parents) or maternal (their mother's parents).
    - ▪ They can ask you or this would be a good time to practice using the telephone and calling the grandparents.
    - ▪ They can still do this if their grandparents are no longer living. It would be a good way to learn about them.

Lesson 113

- Students will: use semicolons in writing, collect information for their autobiography
- The sentence they are imitating today uses semicolons. Have your child find them in the sentence. A semicolon usually acts like a period.
- Lesson 113 worksheet
  - o After they find the semicolons, they are going to write their own sentences.
  - o There are eight pages today in the back of the book for the great grandparents. Your grandparents. Your kids can interview you, but they could also call their grandparents and ask them.

Lesson 114

- Students will: write a story
- Lesson 114 worksheet
  - o Read the directions on the page. There are things they are to include.
  - o If they are stuck, tell them a story about one of your parents or grandparents. They can write that.

Lesson 115 (book)

- Students will: identify paragraphs
- Get out a book and show your child the paragraphs in the book.
  - o Point out how each paragraph begins indented, moved over a little.

- ○ A new paragraph begins when the topic changes. It also changes every time there is a new speaker.
- Lesson 115 worksheet
  - ○ They will be answering questions about paragraphs.
  - ○ There are two autobiography pages (in the back). They are to write about the day they were born.

Lesson 116

- Students will: practice spelling, identify adverbs
- Does your child remember what adverbs are?
  - ○ They describe, or modify, verbs, adjectives, and other adverbs.
    - ▪ Did they very cleverly answer? ☺
- Lesson 116 worksheet
  - ○ There are two parts. The spelling they are supposed to figure out on their own.
  - ○ Then they need to find four adverbs. Two are LY adverbs. The ones that aren't are modifying an adverb and an adjective.

Lesson 117

- Students will: write a story for their autobiography
- Lesson 117 worksheet
  - ○ They should use the page to work on making longer and more interesting sentences.
  - ○ Then there are two autobiographical pages (in the back of the book) about themselves.
    - ▪ They are to describe themselves. It could be adjectives or it could be words like soccer.
    - ▪ The second page is for a story of an important event in their life. This is just a one-day assignment.

Lesson 118

- Students will: practice spelling
- Lesson 118 worksheet
  - ○ Read the words together. These are vocabulary words from Reading 4. If you are using that, you can go over meanings.
  - ○ They need to find the words in the puzzle.

Lesson 119

- Students will: write a story for their autobiography
- Lesson 119 worksheet
  - ○ There is a page on adjectives. There isn't just one right answer for each blank. (continued on the next page)

- o In the back of the book in the autobiography section, they are to write their favorite things and then write a story about them and one of their favorite things. This is just a one-day assignment.

Lesson 120

- Students will: identify parts of speech
  - o How is fallen used in these sentences?
    - The fallen tree is blocking the road.
      - adjective
    - The tree has fallen across the road.
      - verb
    - On Memorial Day we remember the fallen.
      - noun
- Lesson 120 worksheet
  - o They need to pay attention to how the words are used in a sentence.

Lesson 121

- Students will: answer questions about a book they've read
- Lesson 121 worksheet
  - o There are questions on the page about a book. They are to answer a bunch of them. They should fill the lines given.

Lesson 122

- Students will: write a book review
- Lesson 122 worksheet
  - o They need to write a paragraph to review the book they answered questions about on Lesson 121.
    - They need to add an intro and conclusion and make sure to include the title of the book and a short summary of its plot, in one sentence if possible.

Lesson 123

- Students will: identify parts of speech, continue work on their autobiography
- Lesson 123 worksheet
  - o They need to look at how the words are used in the sentences.
  - o There is an autobiography page for today (in the back) about places they have lived. If they have only lived in one home, they could include places they have spent any significant time, like a grandparent's home or info about your home town.

Lesson 124

- Students will: write a story for their autobiography, practice editing and describing
- Lesson 124 worksheet
  - There are editing and description activities on the page for them to practice with.
  - There is a page in the back of the book for the autobiography. What is the story of their life? That's what goes here. They can take some time to finish on Lesson 125 if it's taking a long time. You can staple on more pages if need be.

Lesson 125

- Students will: write, conduct an interview
- They can work on finishing their life story if need be.
- Lesson 125 worksheet
  - They are to interview an older family member and take notes. There are directions on the page.
    - They are going to be writing a biographical essay where they give three examples that show a word that describes the person. They should think about what word describes the person.

Lesson 126

- Students will: write a paragraph
- Lesson 126 worksheet
  - They are going to write the first paragraph of the body of the biographical essay. My example in on their page.
    - It needs to start with the main idea. Think hamburger.
    - The paragraph is about the descriptive word and one way it applies to the person.

Lesson 127

- Students will: write a paragraph
- Lesson 127 worksheet
  - They are going to write the second paragraph of the body of the biographical essay. My example in on their page.

Lesson 128

- Students will: write a paragraph
- Lesson 128 worksheet
  - They are going to write the third paragraph of the body of the biographical essay. My example is on their page.

Lesson 129

- Students will: write a paragraph
- Lesson 129 worksheet
  - They are going to write the conclusion paragraph of the biographical essay. My example in on their page.

Lesson 130

- Students will: review grammar
- Lesson 130 worksheet
  - This is a multiple choice exercise of some general language arts concepts.

Lesson 131

- Students will: write a paragraph
- Ask your child if they remember what goes into an introduction paragraph.
  - The first sentence is supposed to make the reader interested, curious. Can they say something clever, funny, surprising?
  - The last sentence is the thesis, the main idea. It should lead into what's coming in the body paragraphs.
- Lesson 131 worksheet
  - They are going to write the introduction paragraph of the biographical essay. My example is on their page.

Lesson 132

- Students will: edit their essay
- Lesson 132 worksheet
  - There is an editing page for their biographical essay.
  - They should also read it out loud.
  - This would be a nice one to type up to create a final draft. It could be read to the person they wrote about if possible.
  - They are also finished with their autobiography. You can decide if you want to leave it in the book or take it out and put it all together with their biographical essay as well with a cover and everything.

Lesson 133

- Students will: review capitalization, practice spelling
- Ask your child what words in a sentence need to be capitalized.
  - The first letter in each sentence and each name. It could be the name of a person, a place, or a thing.
    - The University of Maryland is capitalized because it's the name of a school.

- If we were talking about a university in Maryland, we would not capitalize university because it's a thing, not the name of a thing. Maryland is always capitalized because it's the name of a place, a state in America.
- Lesson 133 worksheet
  - There are two parts, looking for capitals and putting together syllables to make words.
    - If they are stuck on making words, encourage them to just start saying the syllables together out loud until one sounds right.
    - They can do the ones that are easier for them first and then come back to any others.
    - When you are correcting capitalization, just tell them what sentence has a mistake and see if they can figure out which word is wrong. Can they tell you why?

Lesson 134

- Students will: write an introductory paragraph
- Read this example of an introductory paragraph to your child. (from TTMS.org)
  - It was a humid day in July, the Key Bank sign said that it was 85 degrees outside. That lesson my mom drove me to The Smithfield Theater. I had an important job to do. The job was more of a personal goal. It was to make people laugh.
  - This was written by a fourth grader. Look at this example together and talk about the answers to these questions.
    - How does the first sentence get you into the story?
    - How does the last sentence give the main idea for the story to follow?
- Lesson 134 worksheet
  - They need to pick an event in their life and write about it. Today they need to write the introduction. How are they going to draw the reader in? How are they going to introduce the main idea?

Lesson 135

- Students will: write their story
- Lesson 135 worksheet
  - They are going to write the main part of their story today. They will be finishing this on Lesson 136.

Lesson 136

- Students will: finish their story and write the conclusion
- Talk to your child about writing in a circle.
  - When you write stories, you need to write in a circle. When we write non-fiction, we finish by restating our main idea. It's sort of like that in a story as well. You finish where you start. You close the circle.

- o Have you ever read a book or watched a movie that left you with the question, "What happened to…?" People don't like that. They want to know what happened. They want all the loose ends tied up.
- o Did you ever read a book or watch a movie where at the end it tells you what happened to each character? That's because they know people want the circle closed, they want the loose ends tied up, they want everything settled and everyone happy ☺
- o In the sample story opening from lesson 134 he says he wants to make people laugh. In the end he says he knows he wants to be a comedian. They are saying the same thing. He closes the circle. It makes us happy.

- Lesson 136 worksheet
  - o On lesson 134 you read an example written by a kid who wanted to make people laugh. In the last sentence in his story, the last sentence of his last paragraph, he tells the reader he wants to be a comedian.
  - o Maybe one way to make a circle would be to think about the next time you're going to get to do whatever you wrote about or how you'll always remember that day.
  - o They need to finish their story. Can they make their last sentence leave you with a warm and fuzzy feeling?

Lesson 137

- Students will: edit their story
- Lesson 137 worksheet
  - o There is a checklist for editing. Once they are sure it's technically correct, they should read it out loud and change anything that sounds awkward or that makes them stumble.
  - o They should combine sentences anywhere there are three short sentences next to each other.
  - o They should add adjectives and adverbs.
  - o They should make longer sentences with commas and clauses.
  - o Don't let them say it's good the way it is! They must change it. That's the assignment today. Make it better.
  - o They could make a final draft and save this for their portfolio.

Lesson 138

- Students will: write a main idea sentence, identify adverbs
- Lesson 138 worksheet
  - o They need to pick a story they have recently read or one they know well and write the plot of it, the main idea of what it's about in one sentence.
  - o They need to pick out the adverbs. A couple of them are not LY words. They need to think carefully.

Lesson 139

- Students will: identify adverbs
- Lesson 139 worksheet
  - They just need to underline the adverb that describes the verb.
  - You could save this for their portfolio.

Lesson 140

- Students will: identify adverbs, write introduction and main idea sentences
- Lesson 140 worksheet
  - They are to write about what they read today (or recently).
    - What would be the main idea of the chapter?
    - What would be an interesting way to start talking about the story?

Lesson 141

- Students will: understand the main idea
- The main idea is the point of the paragraph. The details in a paragraph point to the main idea. While paragraphs most often begin with the main idea, there are different types of paragraphs and some end with the main idea. Sometimes the main idea is even in the second sentence.
- Lesson 141 worksheet
  - They need to answer the questions about the main idea.
  - Make sure you check this right away so they can learn from any mistakes. Mistakes are a chance to learn. Mistakes are opportunities!

Lesson 142

- Students will: make inferences
- They are going to be making inferences, educated guesses. A good writer doesn't just tell you things straight out. They show you things.
- Lesson 142 worksheet
  - They are going to choose from the options what they can infer from the story given. What is being shown?

Lesson 143

- Students will: write a main idea sentence, make inferences
- If you saw in a movie or read in a book how the whole family was coming over and they had been cooking a turkey all day, what might you infer?
  - It's Thanksgiving.
- Lesson 143 worksheet
  - They are going to write a one-sentence summary giving the main idea of the chapter they read today or of a story they know well (any chapter, children's book, movie, TV episode).
  - There are also some stories they are supposed to infer something from.

Lesson 144

- Students will: choose the correct verb
- Lesson 144 worksheet
    - They should be able to do this just by the sound of it. If they get any wrong, make sure to have them read the correct sentence out loud, and make sure your family is normally using the correct words.

Lesson 145

- Students will: write past tense verbs
- Lesson 145 worksheet
    - Just like Lesson 144, if they get one wrong, make sure to have them read the correct sentence out loud, and make sure your family is normally using the correct words.

Lesson 146

- Students will: choose the correct verb
- Lesson 146 worksheet
    - Just like Lesson 144, if they get one wrong, make sure to have them read the correct sentence out loud, and make sure your family is normally using the correct words.

Lesson 147

- Students will: write verbs and adverbs
- Hopefully your child knows what action verbs and adverbs are. They will have to write them today. They get to make up whatever they want.
- Lesson 147 worksheet
    - They need to list ten action verbs and then match them with adverbs. Encourage them to have fun with it. You can brainstorm together if they are slow to get started.

Lesson 148

- Students will: write a creative story
- Lesson 148 worksheet
    - They are to write a story using at least five of their verb/adverb combinations. Encourage them to have fun with it and be creative.
    - Give them a high five and/or hug if they use more than five. Maybe you could offer a reward for figuring out how to include them all!

Lesson 149

- Students will: distinguish between homophones

- Ask your child to tell you what kinds of twos there are.
  - There's the number two.
  - There's going to the store.
  - There's, "I want to go too."
    - Point out the spelling of each.
- Ask them to think about the different kinds of there. How many can they think of?
  - It's over there.
  - This is their dog.
  - They're our friends.
    - Point out the spelling of each. Ask what the contraction they're is short for?
      - They are.
      - That's one way to make sure you are using the correct spelling, ask if it means they are.
- Last one, can they think of two different kinds of whose?
  - Whose bike is this?
  - Who's going with us?
    - Point out the spelling and ask what the contraction stands for.
      - who is
- Lesson 149 worksheet
  - They need to fill in the blanks with the correct choice of each of these words.

Lesson 150

- Students will: write specific verbs
- Today they are going to work on improving their writing by coming up with specific verbs. For instance, instead of saying someone walked loudly across the room, you could say they stomped across the room. The specific verb gives a good image of what's going on. Instead of saying someone ran fast across the room, you could say he sprinted across the room.
- Lesson 150 worksheet
  - They are going to write five of the adverb/verb combos and then write a specific verb that could replace it.
  - Then there are other combos on the page they can write a specific verb for. It might be easiest to start with these to get the juices flowing.

Lesson 151 (blue, green, yellow, red, and orange colored pencils or crayons if possible)

- Students will: identify parts of speech
- Lesson 151 worksheet
  - They just need to identify the part of speech of each word. They can match the cherries to the trees by coloring the tree and the cherries for the tree the same color or by coming up with some pattern such as stripes, spots, blank, and colored in if they just have a pencil to use.

Lesson 152

- Students will: identify vowel sounds and adverbs
- Lesson 152 worksheet
  - They need to read the words out loud and listen for the same vowel sound. They are not spelled the same or even written with the same vowels. It's about the sounds.
  - They need to identify the adverbs at the bottom of the page. They need to remember that adverbs can describe adjectives and other adverbs as well as verbs.

Lesson 153

- Students will: identify common and proper nouns
- Lesson 153 worksheet
  - This is a review. The most important thing about this is to remember that when you write names they need to be capitalized.

Lesson 154 (book)

- Students will: write a creative story
- They need to pick five words in a row from a book they are reading now and use that in their story. That's their writing prompt. You can choose for them if you like.
- Lesson 154 worksheet
  - They need to write a story and read it to you or an audience.

Lesson 155

- Students will: practice spelling
- Lesson 155 worksheet
  - Give them their words.
    - kitchen
    - staircase
    - instrument
    - ornament
    - shoreline
    - purchase
    - burden
    - surgeon
    - executive
    - judicial
    - legislative
    - jurisdiction
  - Remember to not just give them the correct spelling. Help them think it through and then have them write the whole word correctly, not just fix the mistake.

Lesson 156

- Students will: edit sentences, identify sentence types
- Ask your child to tell you the type of sentence and how it is punctuated.
  - declarative
    - makes a statement, ends with a period
  - interrogative
    - asks a question, ends with a question mark
  - imperative
    - makes a demand, ends with a period or exclamation point
  - exclamatory
    - exclaims something, ends in an exclamation point
- Lesson 156 worksheet
  - They are going to be correcting capitalization and punctuation along with identifying the sentence type.

Lesson 157

- Students will: identify correct homophones and homonyms
- Lesson 157 worksheet
  - They need to do the best they can in figuring out which homophone to use. They need to think about which each one means and which seems spelled right for the meaning needed.
  - Then they need to write the homonym described by the sentences.

Lesson 158

- Students will: write a story using homophones
- Here are some homophones for inspiration.
  - aisle, I'll
  - allowed, aloud
  - ant, aunt
  - ate, eight
  - bare, bear
- Lesson 158 worksheet

Lesson 159

- Students will: write a friendly letter
- You can refer to Lesson 60, but that's a business letter.
- Here's the friendly letter format. It is basically similar.
  - They will write a heading at the top. That can be the date.
  - Then they need their salutation, the Dear Mom part. It starts with a capital letter and is followed by a comma.

- Then there's the body. It can just be one sentence, but you don't have to tell them that.
- Then the closing, the Sincerely, Love, etc. That is also capitalized and also followed by a comma.
- The last line is the signature, or the name printed.
- Lesson 159 worksheet
  - There are lines on the page for each part of the letter.

Lesson 160

- Students will: write an acrostic poem
- They need to pick a topic. If they don't have one, they can do their birth month, or their name, or someone's name in your family, or a pet's name…
- Lesson 160 worksheet
  - They are to write their topic word one letter on each line down the page.
  - Then they write something about the topic with each line starting with a word that begins with the letter on the line.
  - There's an example on the page.

Lesson 161

- Students will: write a description
- Their worksheet gives them a sentence to start with. They are to imagine a scene and describe it. There's no story, no plot, just a picture. Here's my example.
  - The wind blew cold and dry. Leaves tumbled across the parking lot, scraping the pavement with their crisp, dry edges. One lonely car, accompanied only by a trash dumpster, sat in the corner of the empty lot. It huddled under the balding tree. The sky was clear blue like an untouched pool of summer, but the cold wind reminded that summer was past.
- Lesson 161 worksheet
  - They are to write one paragraph, at least five sentences.

Lesson 162

- Students will: describe a character
- They are going to add a character to their scene. They aren't rewriting what they wrote. That would come first in the story to set the scene. Then a character comes into the scene. They need to think very specifically about the character and what they are like and describe him, her, or it. This is still description. The focus is not on anything happening. You are still describing what you see in your scene.
- Here's my example.
  - A dog came traipsing across the lot. He was scruffy and unkempt but had a spring in his step and a smile on his face. He wasn't starved; he had muscle on his bones. He was a mutt, a mix of this and that and probably, the other as well. He was nondescript — not big, not small, his fur not long, not short. He had spots of black and brown and probably at one time white.

- What do you know about the character from the description? What might you infer?
    - He's a stray (dirty) but he knows how to get around and get what he needs (not hungry). He's smiling. He's walking like he owns the world.
- Lesson 162 worksheet
    - They are to write one paragraph, at least five sentences.

Lesson 163

- Students will: write an action sequence
- They are going to be continuing their story. They've described a setting and a character. Now something totally unexpected is going to happen and they will write how that impacts the setting and character.
- Here's my example.
    - The dog bounded onto the car and into the dumpster, nose first. He didn't reappear at first. You would expect that he was scrounging for a tasty morsel, a leftover from an over-picky child. But when he leaped from the dumpster, he was barely the same dog! He was wearing sunglasses and a black leather coat! He popped open the car door with his nose, hopped in, and started the car. He was a spy dog!
- Lesson 163 worksheet
    - They have the directions on the page. They need to make it unexpected. Brainstorm together if this is stressful instead of fun.
    - On Lesson 164 they will write an ending.

Lesson 164

- Students will: write an ending
- Lesson 164 worksheet
    - Here's my example.
        - He spun the car around and spotted me. As he drove past, he winked at me and said, "You didn't see anything."
        - Did my ending make you smile?
    - Challenge your child: Can you make your audience feel something?

Lesson 165

- Students will: edit, present a story
- They need to edit their work. Make sure they read it out loud to listen for awkward phrases or poor transitions.
- Do they need to add transitions?
- Can they add similes? Can they add adjectives, adverbs, better words?
- Lesson 165 worksheet
    - There's an editing checklist here for them.
    - They could type up a final draft if they like their story.
    - They need to read it to an audience.

Lesson 166 (You might want to get to the library today or in the next couple of days to get books on the topic.)

- Students will: review grammar, choose a research topic
  - They need to pick a topic to research. Ideally this would be related to something they have studied this year in science or history.
- Lesson 166 worksheet
  - They need to correct the paragraph. They need to look for punctuation, spelling, word choice and capitalization corrections.

Lesson 167

- Students will: research their topic
- Lesson 167 worksheet
  - They need to record their resources and take notes on facts. There are directions on the page for the best way to take notes. They aren't to copy sentences.

Lesson 168

- Students will: research their topic
- Lesson 168 worksheet
  - They need to record their resources and take notes on facts.

Lesson 169

- Students will: research their topic
- Lesson 169 worksheet
  - They need to record their resources and take notes on facts.

Lesson 170

- Students will: write their introduction
- Here are my previous directions on writing an introduction.
  - You are going to write an introduction for your research report. It needs to be at least three sentences long.
  - The last sentence is going to be your main idea. It will tell the main idea of your research report. It should be as specific as is possible.
  - Your first sentence should be interesting. It should make people want to read your biography. An easy way to get people interested is by asking them a question. Other ways include using a quote, making an interesting observation, or saying something funny.
- Lesson 170 worksheet
  - They are to write one paragraph. Make sure the first sentence peeks curiosity and the last states the main idea.

Lesson 171 (Five different colors or colored pencil or crayon)
- Students will: organize facts
- Lesson 171 worksheet
  - Read the directions on the page together.
  - They need to see what related facts they have. Think about five groups of facts. There needs to be more than one fact for there to be a group.

Lesson 172

- Students will: make an outline
- Lesson 172 worksheet
  - This isn't an official outline. On the first line they should write introduction. On the last line they need to write conclusion.
  - Then they need to decide on how to order their groups. If they have a ton of facts in a group, they can split it into two groups.
  - They need to write their group names in the order they should go on their page today.
    - Each topic is going to become a paragraph in their report.

Lesson 173

- Students will: write an outline
- Lesson 173 worksheet
  - They are going to put their mini outline into outline form.
  - There are two pages. They may not have that many groups of facts. They need to have at least five (through E).
  - They write the group name by the letter and then facts by the numbers. They only have to have at least two facts for each group.

Lesson 174

- Students will: write two paragraphs
- Lesson 174 worksheet
  - They need to write the first two topic paragraphs for their report.
  - They should use topics A and B from Lesson 173.
  - The first sentence of each paragraph should be a main idea sentence.
  - Can they transition from the first to the second paragraph?

Lesson 175

- Students will: write two paragraphs
- Lesson 175 worksheet
  - They are to write paragraphs for topics C and D.
  - They should think about a transition at the beginning of each new paragraph.
    - also, secondly, not only, …

Lesson 176

- Students will: write a paragraph
- Lesson 176 worksheet
  - They are to finish their topic paragraphs, however many are necessary.
  - Don't forget transitions!

Lesson 177

- Students will: write a conclusion
- Lesson 177 worksheet
  - Read the directions on the page together.

Lesson 178

- Students will: edit their report
- Lesson 178 worksheet
  - They need to check their report for mistakes. There is a checklist on their page.
  - They should read it out loud and change anything that sounds awkward or makes them stumble.
  - If there are several short sentences in a row, they should be combined into longer sentences.
  - You can decide if this should be typed for a final draft.

Lesson 179

- Students will: write a bibliography
- This is how to list books and websites in the bibliography.
  - Last, First M. *Book Title*. City of Publication: Publisher, Year Published. Year Printed.
  - Web site address (date the information was researched)
- Lesson 179 worksheet
  - Each source starts a new line. Do the best you can with the information you have on the resources.

Lesson 180

- Students will: publish and present report
  - Create a final draft if desired.
  - When they are ready, they are to read it to an audience.
- Lesson 180 worksheet
  - There is space for a response from three people.
- Celebrate finishing LA 4!

EP Language Arts 4

Workbook Answers

Lesson 2

Syllables

How many syllables are in the following words? Write the number of syllables in the blank beside the word. If you need help, put your hand under your chin and say the word out loud. The number of times your hand goes down is the number of syllables in the word.

Word	Syllables		Word	Syllables
carrot	2		aquarium	4
burger	2		Philadelphia	5
basketball	3		capitalization	6
umbrella	3		electrifying	5
butterfly	3		encyclopedia	6
airplane	2		Mesopotamia	6
caterpillar	4		mysterious	4
giraffe	2		cantaloupe	3
bottle	2		experience	4
telephone	3		aluminum	4

Lesson 3

Guess the Word

Use the blanks below to guess the words. The words are in the Parent's Guide. You can use the alphabet above each set of blanks to keep track of the letters you've guessed by crossing them out. Can you guess each word before you get 10 missed letters?

A B C D E F G H I J K L M N O P Q R S T U V W X Y Z

T R O U B L E

A B C D E F G H I J K L M N O P Q R S T U V W X Y Z

D E S E R V E

A B C D E F G H I J K L M N O P Q R S T U V W X Y Z

H E L M E T

A B C D E F G H I J K L M N O P Q R S T U V W X Y Z

C O M P U T E R

A B C D E F G H I J K L M N O P Q R S T U V W X Y Z

P E N C I L

Lesson 6

Spelling Bee

Fill in the missing words from the story. The list of words is in the Parent's Guide. Spell each word the best that you can and learn from any mistakes that you make.

We had a wonderful family ___vacation___ to the ___beach___. First, we built sandcastles using our ___shovel___ and ___bucket___. Next, we went on a hunt for sea ___creatures___. My favorite was the ___purple___ sea anemone I found in the shallow tide pool. Finally, we went ___swimming___ in the ___ocean___. We practically ___floated___ in all of that salt!

Lesson 8

Word Builder

How many words can you make from the letters in the box below? Only use letters that are adjacent to each other (see the example).

B	R	A	S	B	L	A	K
N	I	S	H	E	U	C	Y
O	S	H	G	D	J	K	S
K	B	G	I	L	O	N	P
L	M	Q	U	S	W	Y	A
I	N	O	E	P	T	K	S
O	L	E	S	R	D	B	T
F	I	H	T	C	F	H	M
C	E	D	U	E	W	T	A
A	R	G	L	L	Z	Y	T
N	L	H	S	M	A	E	E
B	W	A	Y	R	G	F	D
E	D	O	T	U	K	T	E
P	R	L	C	N	D	G	F

(Answers will vary. Some options include the following.)

brains	black
blue	she
quest	queen
maze	ways
shade	nose
grace	nest

Lesson 9

Noun Review

Remember that a noun is a person, place, thing, or idea. Color in the clouds below that contain nouns.

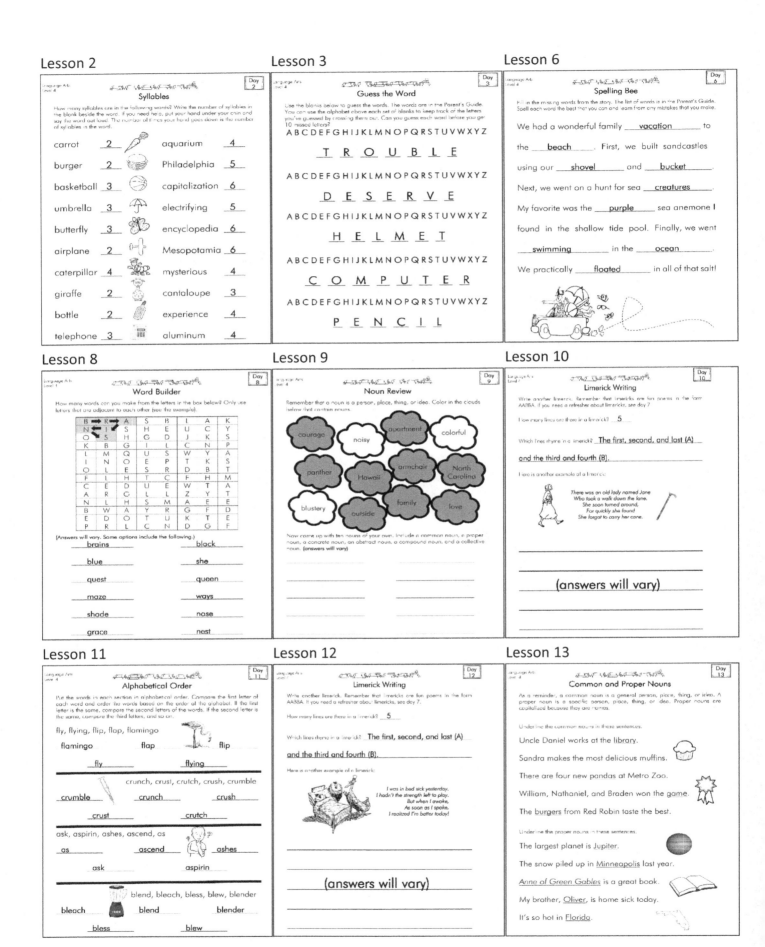

(clouds: courage, noisy, apartment, colorful, panther, Hawaii, armchair, North Carolina, blustery, outside, family, love)

Now come up with ten nouns of your own. Include a common noun, a proper noun, a concrete noun, an abstract noun, a compound noun, and a collective noun. (answers will vary)

Lesson 10

Limerick Writing

Write another limerick. Remember that limericks are fun poems in the form AABBA. If you need a refresher about limericks, see day 7.

How many lines are there in a limerick? __5__

Which lines rhyme in a limerick? __The first, second, and last (A) and the third and fourth (B).__

Here is another example of a limerick:

There was an old lady named Jane
Who took a walk down the lane.
She soon turned around,
For quickly she found
She forgot to carry her cane.

(answers will vary)

Lesson 11

Alphabetical Order

Put the words in each section in alphabetical order. Compare the first letter of each word and order the words based on the order of the alphabet. If the first letter is the same, compare the second letters of the words. If the second letter is the same, compare the third letters, and so on.

fly, flying, flip, flap, flamingo

flamingo	flap	flip
fly	flying	

crunch, crust, crutch, crush, crumble

crumble	crunch	crush
crust	crutch	

ask, aspirin, ashes, ascend, as

as	ascend	ashes
ask	aspirin	

blend, bleach, bless, blew, blender

bleach	blend	blender
bless	blew	

Lesson 12

Limerick Writing

Write another limerick. Remember that limericks are fun poems in the form AABBA. If you need a refresher about limericks, see day 7.

How many lines are there in a limerick? __5__

Which lines rhyme in a limerick? __The first, second, and last (A) and the third and fourth (B).__

Here is another example of a limerick:

I was in bed sick yesterday.
I hadn't the strength left to play.
But when I awoke,
As soon as I spoke,
I realized I'm better today!

(answers will vary)

Lesson 13

Common and Proper Nouns

As a reminder, a common noun is a general person, place, thing, or idea. A proper noun is a specific person, place, thing, or idea. Proper nouns are capitalized because they are names.

Underline the common nouns in these sentences.

Uncle Daniel works at the library.

Sandra makes the most delicious muffins.

There are four new pandas at Metro Zoo.

William, Nathaniel, and Braden won the game.

The burgers from Red Robin taste the best.

Underline the proper nouns in these sentences.

The largest planet is Jupiter.

The snow piled up in Minneapolis last year.

Anne of Green Gables is a great book.

My brother, Oliver, is home sick today.

It's so hot in Florida.

Lesson 14

Action Verbs

Remember that action verbs tell what someone or something does or is doing. Color in the flip flops below that contain action verbs.

flying • jump • sail • computer • dance • swim • swallow • frustrated • colorful • spinning • necklace • falling • read • driving

Now come up with ten action verbs of your own. **(Answers will vary)**

Lesson 15

Writing

Read these first two stanzas of the poem Speak Gently:

Speak gently; it is better far
To rule by love than fear;
Speak gently; let no harsh words mar
The good we might do here.

Speak gently to the little child;
Its love be sure to gain;
Teach it in accents soft and mild;
It may not long remain.

What form, or rhyme scheme, is the poem written in? **ABAB**

How many syllables are in each line? **8, 6, 8, 6**

Write a poem with two stanzas following the same format.

(answers will vary)

Lesson 16

Spelling Bee

Fill in the missing words from the story. The list of words is in the Parent's Guide. Spell each word the best that you can and learn from any mistakes that you make.

The Kentucky Derby has been __called__ the "most __exciting__ two minutes in sports." This title refers to the time it takes the __horses__ to complete their run around the track. Bigger than most races, the Derby features __twenty__ horses running like the wind around the track in an attempt to win the two __million__ dollar prize. The Kentucky Derby takes place on the first __Saturday__ in May and has since 1875. This makes it the __longest__ continually held sporting event in America.

Lesson 18

Spelling

Unscramble the following words. Can you rearrange the letters so that they make actual words? If you need help, look at the definition underneath each word.

UARYLOCBVA — vocabulary
Words and their definitions.

TCRPEMOU — computer
A machine used for storing and processing data.

INECLP — pencil
A writing utensil.

OBULTRE — trouble
Difficulty; problems.

EONUINTC — continue
To keep going.

RENTSGTH — strength
Being strong.

EETLHM — helmet
A hard, protective sort of hat.

RVEDSEE — deserve
Be worthy of.

IQYULET — quietly
Without making much noise.

Lesson 19

Action and Linking Verbs

As a reminder, an action verb tells what someone or something does. A linking verb links a subject and predicate without showing action. Underline the verb in each sentence below. On the line beside it, describe the type of verb as either A for action or L for linking.

Sentence	
Her father is a veterinarian.	L
Briley delighted the crowd.	A
The dinner looks tasty.	L
The skaters are fast.	L
My mom paid for my dinner.	A
The boys tossed the football.	A
My writing assignment was long.	L
The girl sighed loudly.	A
We quickly became great friends.	L
Sarah used chopsticks easily.	A
Ezra seems lonely today.	L
The bus arrived later than expected.	A

Lesson 21

Spelling

Listen to your spelling words as they are read to you from the Parent's Guide. All of these words have the oo sound like in the word coop.

scoop • routine • wound • loop • hoop • souvenir • mood • raccoon • troop • food • booth • broom

Lesson 23

Spelling

Fill in the blanks with the spelling words that best fit the sentence. All of these words have the OO sound.

I got an extra __s c o o p__ of ice cream.

We practiced our dance __r o u t i n e__ all day.

The roller coaster had a tall __l o o p__.

The nurse bandaged my sister's __w o u n d__.

Daniel shot the ball straight into the __h o o p__.

I bought a __s o u v e n i r__ on our trip.

A __r a c c o o n__ got into our trash can.

My grandmother cooks delicious __f o o d__.

The __t r o o p__ returned safely from deployment.

We had a __b o o t h__ at the craft fair.

I used the __b r o o m__ to clean the kitchen.

Lesson 29

Common and Proper Nouns

Sort the words into the correct box.

Christmas • Monday • park • sandwich • girl • Disneyland • Nashville • rocket • Alaska • Earth • dog • bus

Proper Nouns		Common Nouns	
Christmas	Monday	park	sandwich
Disneyland	Nashville	girl	rocket
Alaska	Earth	dog	bus

Match the proper noun to its common noun by drawing a line between them.

Matthew — boy
Easter — holiday
Friday — day
Mount Rushmore — landmark
June — month
Canada — country

Lesson 31

Handwriting

Write the longest sentence you can find in a book you are reading. Use your very best handwriting and be sure to correctly copy all of the spelling, punctuation, and capitalization.

(answers will vary)

Nouns and Verbs

Underline the proper noun:
My best friend, Patricia, is a gymnast.

Underline the common noun:
The boy was crying when he got hurt.

Underline the linking verb:
You look tired today.

Underline the action verb (any orientation):
Brooke went to dance class yesterday. (dance is describing class)

Lesson 33

Main Idea

Draw a line from the bee to the flower that contains the main idea of each set.

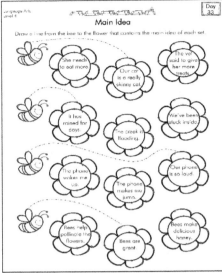

Lesson 34

Main Idea

Read the paragraphs and answer the questions about them.

Remember that main ideas are what the paragraph or story is about. Sometimes they are stated, usually in the first sentence of a paragraph. Sometimes they are unstated and are more of a summary of the whole paragraph.

What is the main idea of this paragraph?
a. Sometimes main ideas are stated.
b. Main ideas are what the paragraph or story is about.
c. Sometimes main ideas are unstated.

Have you ever watched an ice hockey game? It's completely legal to slam people into the boards as hard as possible. People get carried off the ice on stretchers from time to time. Concussions are common in the sport. Perhaps the danger is part of the excitement!

What is the main idea of this paragraph?
a. Ice hockey can be dangerous.
b. Have you ever watched an ice hockey game?
c. Stretchers are involved in some hockey games.

Bristol has a beautiful flower garden. She has a huge array of flowers including roses and carnations. She takes great care of her flowers and waters them daily. Flowers fill her with joy.

What is the main idea of this paragraph?
a. Bristol waters her flowers every day.
b. Roses and carnations are types of flowers.
c. Bristol really likes flowers.

My brother is so silly. His favorite food is mashed potatoes and ketchup. He wears a cape everywhere he goes. He twirls his hand above his head and runs down the hallways yelling, "yeehaw!" multiple times a day. He's crazy, but I love him.

What is the main idea of this paragraph?
a. I have a silly brother.
b. My brother likes weird food combinations.
c. My brother wears a cape everywhere he goes.

Lesson 36

Handwriting

Copy a great sentence from a book you are reading — something exciting, interesting, descriptive, or funny. Write carefully and neatly.

(answers will vary)

Main Idea

Read the paragraphs and choose the main idea of each one.

Samuel is a kind-hearted kid. He donated his birthday money to the local homeless shelter when he learned he wasn't old enough to serve there. He swept his neighbor's porch when she twisted her ankle. He kept his dad from squishing a spider, convincing him to set it free outside instead. Samuel is a joy to be around.

What is the main idea of this paragraph?
a. Samuel donated money to the homeless.
b. Samuel is compassionate.
c. Samuel likes spiders.

Apples are a great snack choice. They are full of fiber and vitamin C. The polyphenols in apples act as antioxidants. Everything from your bones to your brain can benefit from eating apples.

What is the main idea of this paragraph?
a. Your bones can benefit from apples.
b. Apples are good for you.
c. Apples have polyphenols.

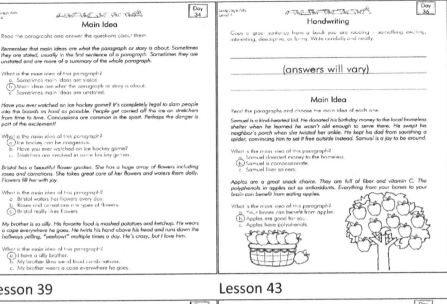

Lesson 38

Spelling

Find the words in the puzzle below. Words can be found forward, backward, up, down, and diagonally.

vocabulary	computer	pencil
trouble	continue	strength
helmet	deserve	quietly

Lesson 39

Reading Comprehension

Read the story below and then answer the questions about the story.

The Fox and the Stork

At one time the Fox and the Stork were on visiting terms and seemed very good friends. So the Fox invited the Stork to dinner, and for a joke put nothing before her but some soup in a very shallow dish. This the Fox could easily lap up, but the Stork could only wet the end of her long bill in it, and left the meal as hungry as when she began. "I am sorry," said the Fox, "the soup is not to your liking."

"Pray do not apologize," said the Stork. "I hope you will return this visit, and come and dine with me soon." So a day was appointed when the Fox should visit the Stork; but when they were seated at table all that was for their dinner was contained in a very long-necked jar with a narrow mouth, in which the Fox could not insert his snout, so all he could manage to do was to lick the outside of the jar.

"I will not apologize for the dinner," said the Stork: "One bad turn deserves another."

What did the Fox serve for dinner?
a. stork
b. soup in a shallow dish
c. food in a long-necked jar
d. nothing

What did the Stork serve for dinner?
a. fox
b. soup in a shallow dish
c. food in a long-necked jar
d. nothing

Why did the Fox serve what he served?
a. as a joke
b. to be mean
c. they weren't friends
d. foxes don't like storks

What is the moral of the story?
a. Never trust a fox.
b. Storks get even.
c. Foxes and storks can't be friends.
d. One bad turn deserves another.

Lesson 43

Spelling

Write your spelling words on the lines below as they are read to you from the Parent's Guide. Learn from any spelling mistakes you make.

remember	neutral
happened	product
retain	council
mortal	measure
early	utensil
canopy	abundant

Lesson 44

Quotation Marks

Add the missing punctuation to the sentences below by writing it in. Underline words that should be capitalized that aren't. Remember that quotations are punctuated like this:

"Let's have dinner."
"Let's have dinner," he said to her.
He said, "Let's have dinner."

"Will you please turn on the TV?" asked Dad.

"I can't find the remote anywhere," he added.

I asked him, "have you checked under the couch cushions?"

"Sometimes Rex gets ahold of it and buries it there."

Dad replied, "that crazy dog! I didn't think of that."

"Aha! I found it!" he exclaimed after checking the couch cushions.

"Now can you bring me a towel?" he asked.

He grimaced, "he must have hidden it recently. It's still covered in slobber!"

Lesson 49

Quotation Marks

Add the missing punctuation to the sentences below by writing it in. Underline words that should be capitalized that aren't.

"Where have you been, Mom?" asked Jeffrey. "we've been looking all over for you!"

"I'm sorry," answered Mom. "I needed to run an errand. But we can go to the park now."

"Okay, let's go," Rebecca stated. "I want to get there before all of the swings are taken."

Mom replied, "okay. It's a beautiful day for a ride. Should we take the bikes?"

"Yeah!" both Jeffrey and Rebecca exclaimed in unison.

"Do we have any more sunscreen?" asked Jeffrey.

Mom answered, "good call, Jeffrey. Let's get that on now so it can soak in before we get to the park."

"We should also bring some water," said Rebecca. "it's hot out there today."

"You've both been listening during our health unit," remarked Mom proudly.

Lesson 56

Writing

Write an introduction about your biography. This can be a shorter paragraph but should be at least three sentences long. This time instead of the first sentence being your main idea, the last sentence is going to be the main idea of your whole biography. It should be as specific as possible. Make your first sentence interesting. It should make people want to read your biography. An easy way to get people interested is by asking a question.

Proper Nouns

Which of the following nouns are proper? Do you remember?

apple | Mike Pence | coach | Africa | Chicago Cubs | baseball

country | shoulder | Metro Zoo | donut | Florida

penguin | window | Microsoft | Easy Peasy | towel | Jenn

Lesson 58

Writing

Write a conclusion paragraph for your biography. The first sentence should be your main idea again. Like your introduction, there should be at least three sentences. The last sentence should include the word "I." Tell what you think or feel about the person. Answer the question "so who?" Tell why you wrote the essay.

_____

_____

_____

_____

_____

Linking Verbs

Which of the following are linking verbs? Do you remember?

was — hit — zooming — cheer — has been — is
calling — am — are — eating — dribble
look — closed — were — have been — starts — will be

Lesson 59

Nouns

Remember that pronouns take the place of nouns. Which of the words below are pronouns?

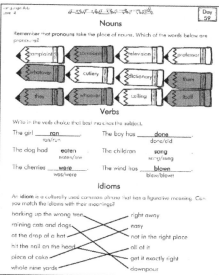

complaint — someone — television — professor
leftover — cutlery — dictionary — them
they — whoever — ceiling — itself

Verbs

Write in the verb choice that best matches the subject.

The girl __ran__ (ran/run)   The boy has __done__ (done/did)

The dog had __eaten__ (eaten/ate)   The children __song__ (song/sung)

The cherries __were__ (was/were)   The wind has __blown__ (blew/blown)

Idioms

An idiom is a culturally used common phrase that has a figurative meaning. Can you match the idioms with their meanings?

barking up the wrong tree — right away
raining cats and dogs — easy
at the drop of a hat — not in the right place
hit the nail on the head — all of it
piece of cake — get it exactly right
whole nine yards — downpour

Lesson 74

Adjectives

Underline the adjectives in the following sentences.

The bright light shined through the clean window.

Sally's purple scarf was made of soft cashmere.

We attended a delectable feast on that sunny Friday.

Our crazy family has a fabulous time together.

Her long, curly hair shimmered red in the sunshine.

The giggly baby lit up with a huge smile.

The sweltering heat sent us all inside for cool air.

Her bubbly bathwater smelled of fragrant lilacs.

His broken radio squawked out horrible sounds.

Have you been to the much-anticipated movie yet?

My favorite sweater is in the dirty laundry.

My annoying hiccups lasted forty-five minutes.

The friendly puppy licked my sticky fingers.

Lesson 76

Adjectives

This fisherman wants a delicious dinner so he only wants you to color in the fish that contain adjectives.

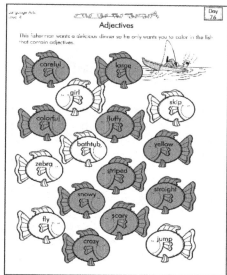

careful — large — girl — skip — colorful — fluffy — yellow — bathtub — zebra — striped — snowy — straight — fly — scary — crazy — jump

---

Lesson 79

Adjectives

Underline the adjectives in the sentences below. In addition to all you've learned about adjectives, keep in mind that the following words are always adjectives: a, an, the, my, our, your, their.

We went to the huge carnival and saw your brother there.

My best friend cooked a delicious meal.

What is your favorite book?

The girl with the blonde hair took my dessert.

Our bouncy ball flew over the privacy fence.

Which of the choices is an adjective? Some sentences have more than one!

You did a fantastic job on your spelling worksheet.
● fantastic   ○ job
○ you   ○ worksheet

The three girls went to see the scary movie yesterday.
○ movie   ○ went
● three   ● scary

Her athletic ability was incredibly impressive.
○ ability   ● athletic
○ was   ● impressive

Our back pond was solid ice.
○ pond   ● back
● our   ● solid

Lesson 84

Parts of Speech

Let's review the parts of speech! Color all of the nouns blue (x-ed). Color all of the verbs green (colored). Color all of the adjectives red (left untouched).

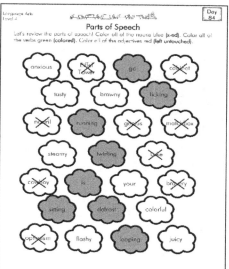

anxious — Eiffel Tower — go — cabinet — tasty — brawny — licking — nostril — running — gorgeous — matchbox — steamy — twirling — bike — cowboy — is — your — brawny — sitting — defrost — colorful — optimism — flashy — leaping — juicy

---

Lesson 88

Spelling

Write your spelling words on the lines below as they are read to you from the Parent's Guide. Learn from any spelling mistakes you make.

building   revise

carefully   scientists

inside   leisure

seizure   rupture

pleasure   vulture

culture   measure

Lesson 89

Writing

Copy this sentence on the lines below. Then underline all the adjectives, circle the verbs, and draw a line through the nouns. And as the three children went home up the hill, Peter hugging the engine, now quite its own self again, Bobbie told, with joyous leaps of the heart, the story of how she had been an Engine-burglar.

And as the three children went home up the hill, Peter hugging the engine, now quite its own self again, Bobbie told with joyous leaps of the heart, the story of how she had been an Engine-burglar.

Fill in the missing punctuation in the sentences below. Underline any words that should be capitalized that aren't.

"It's almost my birthday!" my sister practically shouted.

"We should go to the park today," Jeremy suggested.

I can tell by the flowers, trees, and grass that it's spring.

My mom asked, "where would you like to go for lunch?"

Come up with the best adjective you can to describe these nouns. (Answers will vary)

hair   day

floor   tree

Lesson 93

Homophones

Homophones are words that sound alike but have different meanings. Can you match the word to the correct definition?

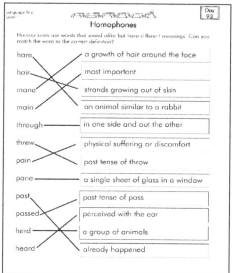

hare — a growth of hair around the face
hair — most important
mane — strands growing out of skin
main — an animal similar to a rabbit
through — in one side and out the other
threw — physical suffering or discomfort
pain — past tense of throw
pane — a single sheet of glass in a window
past — past tense of pass
passed — perceived with the ear
herd — a group of animals
heard — already happened

Lesson 96

Word Builder

How many words can you make from the letters in the box below? Only use letters that are adjacent to each other (see the example).

B	R	A	R	D	A	S	P
N	I	T	I	C	K	A	D
M	S	E	S	A	T	B	O
Z	B	E	T	E	G	N	H
M	C	I	Q	L	R	D	S
A	P	E	E	H	A	C	Y
U	J	P	A	L	Y	O	D
K	R	V	O	E	G	A	D
D	F	I	B	J	T	Q	F
N	O	N	U	T	Z	E	T
C	W	E	K	A	S	C	L
M	B	A	K	G	R	N	E
J	M	D	W	A	F	G	W
L	A	I	T	S	O	E	P

(Answers will vary. Some options include the following.)

brains	rise
vine	bake
yards	none
taken	swag
sick	donut
cards	tricks

Lesson 97

Spelling

Write your spelling words on the lines below as they are read to you from the Parent's Guide. Learn from any spelling mistakes you make.

government   pledge

equation   average

cartridge   knowledge

public   private

academic   athlete

seventy   forty

Lesson 98

Nouns

Can you identify the different noun types? Choose the answer that best describes the word given by filling in the circle beside it.

apples
- ○ singular noun ● plural noun
- ○ proper noun ○ compound noun

Pepsi
- ○ singular noun ○ plural noun
- ○ abstract noun ● proper noun

sunset
- ○ abstract noun ○ plural noun
- ○ proper noun ● compound noun

anxiety
- ● abstract noun ○ plural noun
- ○ collective noun ○ proper noun

vest
- ● singular noun ○ plural noun
- ○ proper noun ○ abstract noun

family
- ○ singular noun ○ proper noun
- ● collective noun ○ plural noun

mice
- ○ singular noun ● plural noun
- ○ abstract noun ○ proper noun

White House
- ○ singular noun ○ plural noun
- ○ abstract noun ● proper noun

Alyssa
- ○ singular noun ○ plural noun
- ● proper noun ○ compound noun

team
- ● collective noun ○ plural noun
- ○ abstract noun ○ proper noun

swimming pool
- ○ abstract noun ○ plural noun
- ○ proper noun ● compound noun

perseverance
- ○ concrete noun ○ plural noun
- ● abstract noun ○ proper noun

Lesson 99

Idioms

Do you know what these idioms mean? Fill in the circle next to the answer you think is correct. Then check your answers and see how you did.

a chip on your shoulder
- ● acting grumpy because you're upset about something
- ○ dropping food on your shirt
- ○ breaking a bone

a dime a dozen
- ○ something that only comes in sets of ten or twelve
- ● something that is very common and easy to get
- ○ something that is cheaply made

tip of the iceberg
- ○ something that sticks up out of nowhere
- ● only a small part of the whole issue
- ○ something sharp

all bark and no bite
- ○ someone who is angry because they are hungry
- ○ a loud dog
- ● someone who has a lot of words but no actions to back it up

break a leg
- ○ have need of first aid
- ● good luck
- ○ to be accident prone

all ears
- ● ready to listen
- ○ not having a sense of smell
- ○ an elephant

Lesson 100

Crossword

Can you fill in the following crossword puzzle? Each matching number equals a matching letter. (For instance, if you thought the "s" belonged in number 1, you would fill in all the number 1s with that letter.) Can you figure it out? Only use letters from the box at the top. They are capitalized for readability. If you need help, look at the hints provided.

F G L N S I W V

Across:
3: move back and forth

Down:
5: go away

Crossword grid:
- A L I V E
- S W I N G
- F L I N G
- S A V E
- L I V E

Lesson 101

Copywork

Copy this sentence: Once on a dark winter's day, when the yellow fog hung so thick and heavy in the streets of London that the shop windows were lighted and the shop windows blazed with gas as they do at night, an odd-looking little girl sat in a cab with her father and was driven rather slowly through the big thoroughfares. Draw a box around all the nouns. Underline all the adjectives. Circle the verbs.

Once on a dark [winter's day], when the yellow [fog]
[hung] so thick and heavy in the [streets] of London that
the [lamps] were (lighted) and the [shop windows] (blazed)
with [gas] as they (do) at night, an odd-looking little [girl]
(sat) in a [cab] with her [father] and (was driven) rather
slowly through the big [thoroughfares].

(Winter's day can be a noun or winter's can be an adjective describing day. Shop windows can be a noun or shop can be an adjective describing windows.) This is a good sentence because it tells what is happening, describes it, and makes you feel it. What types of feelings does this sentence produce?

(Answers will vary)

The adverbs in this sentence are "rather slowly." Adverbs are words that describe verbs, adjectives, and other adverbs. What is the verb being described by rather slowly?

was driven

Lesson 102

Writing

Read this sentence: When Sara entered the school-room the next morning everybody looked at her with wide, interested eyes. List the nouns, adjectives and verbs separately.

Nouns: Sara, school-room, morning, everybody, eyes

Verbs: entered, looked

Adjectives: the, the, next, wide, interested

Write a sentence that shows (not tells) us that the people in the room are scared.

(answers will vary)

Write a sentence that shows (not tells) us that the people in the room are happy.

(answers will vary)

Lesson 103

Writing

Read: On that first morning, when Sara sat at Miss Minchin's side, aware that the whole school-room was devoting itself to observing her, she had noticed very soon one little girl, about her own age, who looked at her very hard with a pair of light, rather dull, blue eyes. List the nouns, pronouns, adjectives, and verbs separately.

Nouns: morning, Sara, Miss Minchin, side, school-room, girl, age, pair, eyes

Pronouns: itself, her, she

Verbs: sat, aware, was devotion, observing, had noticed, looked

Adjectives: that, first, the, whole, one, little, own, a, light, dull, blue

Write a "when" sentence. (Example: When I entered the room, I was surprised by what I saw.)

(Answers will vary)

Add a description to your sentence. (Example: When I entered the room, the one our family spends most of its time in, I was surprised by what I saw.)

(Answers will vary)

Add a clause to the end of your sentence. Don't forget to section off your clauses with commas. (Example: When I entered the room, the one our family spends most of its time in, I was surprised by what I saw, something I will never forget.)

(Answers will vary)

Lesson 106

Parts of Speech

Color the noun apples blue (colored). Color the verb apples red (x'ed). Color the adjective apples green (left untouched).

apple · which · crunchy · chew · crispy · barrel · trade
more · bake · envy · shiny · anger · scratch · these
delicious · smell · goat · bigger · seed · appear · worst

Now write a short story about yourself. Use at least 5 adjectives that describe you.

(answers will vary)

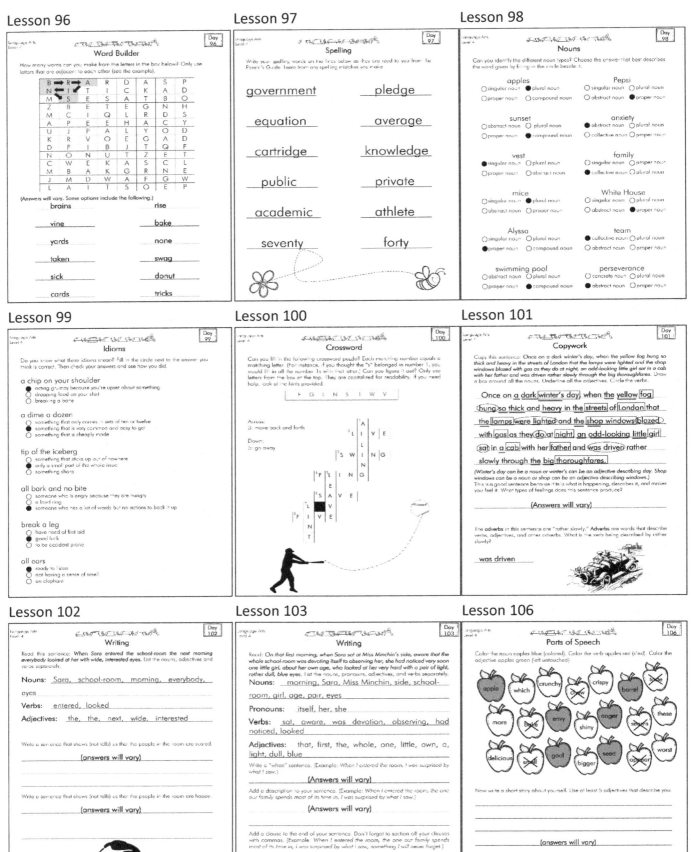

Lesson 107

Adverbs

Write 5 adverbs describing how you can do your school work.

_____
(answers will vary)

Now write 5 adverbs describing how you can treat your family members.

_____
(answers will vary)

Spelling

See how many words you can come up with using the grid of letters below. Only use letters that are adjacent to one another as you have done in the past. This grid is smaller, can you still do it?

C	A	S	E
B	S	L	F
O	T	R	U
P	I	M	E

(answers will vary but might include:)

case	bass	cab(s)
boss	elf	toss
pot(s)	time	fume
sale(s)	flume	trim

Lesson 108

Editing

Fix the errors in the paragraph below by underlining the words that need to be capitalized and correcting the punctuation mistakes.

you've written a lot of short stories so far this year. Have you used lots of adverbs and adjectives to make your stories descriptive? Are your words all spelled correctly? Sometimes spelling mistakes are hard to see. be sure to read carefully! My mom would always ask me, did you punctuate your quotations correctly? Yes, mom, I would answer after checking to be sure. after you've fixed your changes, it can be helpful to have someone else read over your story as well. don't take suggestions as criticisms. Always learn from your mistakes.

Lesson 109

Good vs. Well

The word good is an adjective. It will describe a noun. The word well is an adverb. It will describe a verb, adjective, or other adverb. Can you fill in the blanks below with the correct word?

My grandma cooks really ____well____.

Her picture was drawn so ____well____ I felt like I was in it.

Those donuts tasted really ____good____.

A hot shower feels ____good____ on my muscles.

Do you perform ____well____ under pressure?

Our plans sound ____good____ to me.

Our TV isn't working very ____well____ right now.

A lot of people think Star Wars is a ____good____ series.

How ____well____ are you doing on your school work?

My mother is feeling ____well____ after being sick.

The children put on a ____good____ play at church.

How ____well____ do you know your best friend?

Lesson 112

Spelling

Can you correctly spell the words missing from these sentences? Hint: they all start with the letter b.

I knew he was the sheriff when I saw his **b a d g e**.

I need to fill in the **b l a n k** in this sentence.

The **b e g g a r** asked us for money.

I took my shovel and **b u c k e t** to the beach.

May I **b o r r o w** your pen? Mine ran out of ink.

He blew a large **b u b b l e** with his gum.

Writing

Look at this sentence: When one lives in a row of houses, it is interesting to think of the things which are being done and said on the other side of the wall of the very rooms one is living in. Let's write another "when" sentence. Start with "When ..." At the end of the clause don't forget the comma. For example: When the sun rises, the light warms my body and soul.

_____
(answers will vary)
_____

Lesson 115

Paragraphs

Paragraphs make text easier to read. Each paragraph only deals with one topic or subject. Answer the questions below about paragraphs.

Which of these is a proper paragraph?

I went on a camping trip yesterday. I had a tent, sleeping bag, and flashlight. It was a fun night in the woods.	Sleeping bag	I had a tent, sleeping bag, and flashlight.

How can you use punctuation to show the start of a new paragraph?

Use commas	Indent and start on a new line.	Write in complete sentences.

What would be a reason to start a new paragraph?

A new page	A new sentence	A new topic

In a conversation, what's another reason to start a new paragraph?

A new speaker	A new sentence	It's getting too long

Which of these is split into paragraphs in the right place?

I went on a camping trip yesterday. I had a tent, sleeping bag, and flashlight. The next day, I went home. My bed felt soft.	I went on a camping trip yesterday. I had a tent, sleeping bag, and flashlight. The next day, I went home. My bed felt soft.	I went on a camping trip yesterday. I had a tent, sleeping bag, and flashlight. The next day, I went home. My bed felt soft.

Lesson 116

Spelling

Can you correctly spell the words missing from these sentences? Hint: these words all have the "shun" sound at the end.

We took up a **c o l l e c t i o n** to raise money for the new library.

The road **c o n s t r u c t i o n** for the new bridge made traffic back up for miles.

"One half" is known as a **f r a c t i o n**.

He did a complete **i n s p e c t i o n** of the building to make sure it was safe.

The presidential **e l e c t i o n** draws lots of voters every four years.

Adverbs

Find four adverbs in this sentence. Adverbs answer the question, how. She climbed on a chair, very cautiously raised the skylight, and peeped out. It had been snowing all day, and on the snow, quite near her, crouched a tiny, shivering figure, whose small black face wrinkled itself piteously at sight of her.

____very____   ____cautiously____

____quite____   ____piteously____

Lesson 118

Word Search

Find the words in the word search below. These words are from the book A Little Princess from Easy Peasy's level 4 reading. Words can be found vertically, horizontally, and diagonally.

dexterity	disconsolate	impudent
aperture	precipitately	incontinently
sordid	palpitating	obstinate
rapturous	reconnoiter	importunance

Lesson 119

Adjectives

This story used all the wrong adjectives! Can you replace the negative adjectives with positive ones from the box? Use all of the adjectives once. Some can go in more than one place.

wonderful	available	exhilarating	pleasant	perfect
cheerful	satisfied	delighted	amazing	sunny	terrific

(answers will vary, many words can go different places)

The girls at the park were ____delighted____. The swings
(unhappy)

were ____available____. The sky was ____sunny____
(broken)   (gloomy)

and the air was ____pleasant____, making for a
(crisp)

____wonderful____ day for outside play. The park was
(miserable)

full of ____cheerful____ and ____satisfied____ kids.
(grumpy)   (disgruntled)

"This is so ____amazing____ and ____exhilarating____"
(boring)   (exhausting)

the girls said as they took in the scene. "What a

a ____terrific____ day!"
(horrible)

Lesson 120

Parts of Speech

The barrel at the end of each sentence tells you what part of speech to look for in the sentence. Color in all the apples that should go in that sentence's barrel based on the context of the sentence. Some of them are tricky so pay attention!

Let's go for a relaxing swim in the pool.
go | relaxing | swim | pool → verbs

She went for a run to the bookstore yesterday.
she | run | bookstore | yesterday → nouns

The little girl was overly happy.
the | little | overly | happy → adjectives

The very grumpy man was rudely pouting.
very | grumpy | rudely | pouting → adverbs

She picked up a ball and threw it hard.
She | up | and | (apple) → pronouns

Lesson 123

Parts of Speech

Identify the part of speech of the underlined word and write it on the blank.

Our whole family fit in the <u>enormous</u> booth. **adjective**

The <u>overly</u> luxurious spa weekend was relaxing. **adverb**

"I am excited for Christmas," she <u>said</u> eagerly. **verb**

The large <u>church</u> loomed before us on the hill. **noun**

His pile of books was bigger than <u>mine</u>. **pronoun**

"We <u>are</u> hungry," stated the children. **verb**

Her <u>surprise</u> party was a spectacular success. **adjective**

Come <u>hastily</u> to see the baby bird try to fly! **adverb**

I'm tired. Can we go home <u>soon</u>? **adverb**

The thunderstorm filled my dog with <u>anxiety</u>. **noun**

The cover made the book <u>seem</u> boring. **verb**

Put the book over <u>there</u> on my nightstand. **adverb**

That bathroom isn't going to clean <u>itself</u>. **pronoun**

I find chocolate to be <u>simply</u> irresistible. **adverb**

Lesson 124

Editing

Underline the words that need to be capitalized and add in any missing punctuation to these sentences.

I can't wait! my mom exclaimed eagerly.

We went to <u>seattle</u> in the fall, but it rained our whole trip.

Peter asked, "have you had lunch yet?"

Sheila, Becky, and Sarah joined the soccer team.

"The traffic is bad on lake street," she informed me.

Fill in the blank with a more interesting or more descriptive word than the one that is given. (Answers will vary. These are just examples.)

The flowers are ___**gorgeous**___.
(pretty)

Stacey ___**lobbed**___ the ball.
(threw)

The mouse ___**devoured**___ the cheese.
(ate)

"Get out of my room!" she ___**hollered**___.
(said)

Lesson 130

Grammar Review

Answer the questions below.

This is a person, place, thing, or idea.
(noun)   verb   adjective   adverb

This describes a noun.
noun   verb   (adjective)   adverb

This describes verbs and adjectives.
noun   verb   adjective   (adverb)

This connects the two parts of a compound sentence.
suffix   (conjunction)   synonym   antonym

"Pittsburgh" is an example of this.
(proper noun)   pronoun   linking verb   action verb

"Overly expensive" is an example of this.
(adverb describing an adjective)   homonym
compound sentence   adjective describing a noun

A sentence that makes a command is this type of sentence.
interrogative   declarative   exclamatory   (imperative)

Which part of speech is the underlined word: "I am hungry."?
noun   (verb)   adjective   adverb

Lesson 133

Capitalization

Underline the words in the sentences that should be capitalized.

Will you be coming home for <u>christmas</u> this year?

Both <u>english</u> and <u>french</u> are spoken by <u>canadians</u>.

<u>i</u> went to <u>target</u> to look for some <u>jif</u> peanut butter.

<u>my</u> mother is a graduate of <u>trevecca nazarene university</u>.

<u>i</u> can't believe <u>mrs. moga</u> moved to <u>santa fe</u>!

We all went to <u>holiday world</u> in <u>santa claus, indiana</u>.

Spelling

Join the syllable given with a syllable from the box to make a two syllable word. They are each used only one time.

-day	-ment	-dle	-ful	-dle	-ner	-low	-lete

ath _**lete**_   mid _**dle**_

fig _**ment**_   to _**day**_

din _**ner**_   rest _**ful**_

yel _**low**_   han _**dle**_

Lesson 138

Writing

Write a main idea sentence for the chapter you read today. If you didn't read a chapter today, you'll have to use something else like a children's book you know well or some other story.

_____

_____

_____

Adverbs

Color in the basketballs below that contain adverbs.

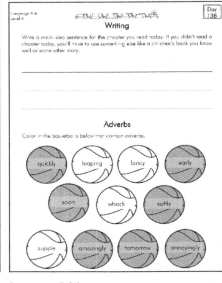

quickly · leaping · fancy · early · soon · whack · softly · supple · amazingly · tomorrow · annoyingly

Lesson 139

Adverbs

Adverbs can tell how something happened. Sally accidentally dropped her doll in the puddle. Adverbs can tell when something happened. Sally dropped her doll yesterday. Adverbs can tell where something happened. Sally dropped it here. Read these sentences. An action verb is in bold type. Underline the adverb that describes the bolded verb.

We <u>quickly</u> **ran** to the mini mart for a snack.

Sandra, will you please **come** <u>here</u>?

We **went** to the park <u>yesterday</u>.

She <u>cautiously</u> **maneuvered** into traffic.

Her daughter **prayed** <u>beautifully</u> before they all ate.

They will **go** to the library <u>soon</u>.

He <u>carefully</u> **wrote** in his best handwriting.

The dog next door <u>always</u> **barks**.

We <u>frantically</u> **searched** for the lost set of keys.

Let's **make** plans <u>tomorrow</u>.

Bonus: My dad **snored** <u>loudly</u> as he **slept** <u>dreamlessly</u>.

Lesson 140

Writing

Write an interesting first sentence for a paragraph in your reading today. Then write a main idea sentence for the chapter you read today. If you don't have a reading assignment today, use something you've read recently or a book you know well.

_____

(answers will vary)

_____

(answers will vary)

Adverbs

Underline the adverbs that describe the bolded verbs below.

The boys <u>exuberantly</u> **played** their hockey game.

I <u>never</u> **see** stars in our bright city sky.

We are **going** to the zoo <u>tomorrow</u>.

Lesson 141

Main Idea

Can you answer these questions about a written piece's main idea? Check your answers when you're finished and review what you missed so you can learn.

A main idea is...
a. the general topic
(b) the specific point being made about the topic
c. a supporting detail

The main idea is reinforced by...
(a) supporting details
b. statements of opinion
c. good grammar

What might be the main idea in an essay on smoking?
a. smoking
b. cigarettes
(c) smoking is bad for your health

Where is the main idea most often in a paragraph?
(a) in the first sentence
b. in the middle
c. in the last sentence

What's a good way to find the main idea of something you're reading?
(a) ask yourself general questions about what you've read
b. only read the piece once
c. memorize the piece

Which statement is true about main ideas?
a. they are always factual
(b) they need to have good supporting details
c. they should be stated first

Lesson 142

Inferences

An **inference** is a guess you can make based on the information you have. It's what some people call reading between the lines. What can you infer from the following passages?

Sheila shivered and checked the thermostat. She turned the heat up a notch and pulled her blanket tighter around herself. She checked that the fire in the fireplace had plenty of kindling to keep burning.
a. Sheila was good at solving problems.
(b) Sheila was cold.
c. It was summer.

I jumped into the pool, a grin lighting up my face.
a. I was being chased by bees.
b. Someone was in trouble and I was a lifeguard.
(c) I was having fun at the pool.

Cam flipped through his scrapbook and smiled. He saw the group picture in front of the Leaning Tower of Pisa. He grinned at the picture of himself in front of Buckingham Palace. He could almost smell the pastries as he gazed on the photo of the Eiffel Tower. It had been a great summer.
a. Cam likes pictures.
b. Cam likes smiling.
(c) Cam took a summer trip to Europe.

I saw a flash of light. Shortly after that, I heard a rumble. The sun seems to have disappeared. Can you predict what might happen next?
a. I will see a great fireworks show in the sky.
b. I will go to sleep because it is nighttime.
(c) It will rain.

Lesson 143

Writing

Write a main idea sentence for the chapter you read today. If you didn't have a reading assignment, use a story you know well.

_____
_____(answers will vary)_____
_____

Inferences

What can you infer from the following? (ANSWERS WILL VARY. SUGGESTIONS:)

It's cold outside. I heard the song *Jingle Bells* at the mall while I shopped for the perfect gift for my brother. Every house has decorative lights adorning the outside. There's a tree in my living room.

_____It's Christmas._____

I baked a dozen cookies last night. There are only two cookies left and I have a horrible stomach ache.

_____I ate all the cookies._____

Rex is my best friend. He wags his tail whenever he sees me. Rex loves to play fetch and has learned to sit, stay, roll over, beg, and shake. He loves it when I scratch his belly.

_____Rex is a dog._____

Lesson 144

Linking Verbs

Fill in the sentences below with the correct present tense linking verb from the box.

| am   is   are |

Your brother __is__ fishing with his friends.

Katie and Stacey __are__ eating lunch in the park.

My mom __is__ feeling poorly today.

You __are__ going to need a coat if you go outside.

I __am__ tossing the football after dinner.

Fill in the sentences below with the correct past tense linking verb from the box.

| were   was |

We __were__ running a marathon this past weekend.

His parents __were__ renewing their vows last Saturday.

She __was__ cheering loudly when her team won.

I __was__ sailing on the lake when the storm came up.

You __were__ singing so beautifully this morning.

Lesson 145

Verbs

Not all past tense verbs end in -ed. In the blank, fill in the past tense form of the verb in parentheses.

The wind __blew__ hard all night long.
(to blow)

The airplane had __flown__ past the runway.
(to fly)

We all __came__ running when we heard the crash.
(to come)

We __lit__ a candle in honor of our grandmother.
(to light)

The choir __sang__ beautifully this morning.
(to sing)

She __brought__ me home from the dentist.
(to bring)

I __wrote__ an essay about Abraham Lincoln.
(to write)

My father __ran__ all the way to the finish line.
(to run)

She was __driven__ to the hospital in an ambulance.
(to drive)

Lesson 146

Verbs

Choose the correct verb apple to fit on the tree.

My shoes and socks (are/am) wet from the rain.

(Don't/Doesn't) you know the answer?

What goes around (come/comes) around.

Both of my parents (are/is) home.

He (run/runs) 6 miles every day.

My fingernails all (have/has) polish on them.

Lesson 149

Grammar

Choose the correct word from the box to fill in the blank.

| two   to   too |

We are going __to__ the concert tonight.

We have __two__ extra tickets.

Maybe Grandma and Grandpa can come, __too__.

They like __to__ go __to__ bed early, though.

| whose   who's |

Do you know __whose__ jacket was left here?

Is it someone __who's__ going to be mad it's lost?

__Who's__ going to make sure it's returned?

| their   them   they're |

We need to return them to __their__ home.

It's across the street over __there__.

They might be in trouble if __they're__ late.

Lesson 151

Parts of Speech

Color the nouns blue, the pronouns yellow, the adjectives red, and the adverbs orange. (Cherries are arranged by their corresponding tree.)

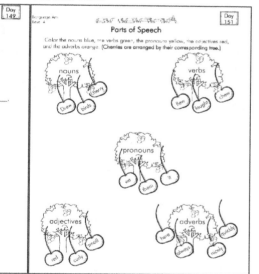

Lesson 152

Vowel Sounds

Write the word from the box that has the same vowel sound as, but different spelling pattern from, the one given.

| said   tweet   flop   loop |
| eye   sail   boat   from |

jump __from__   smile __eye__

nest __said__   pane __sail__

blue __loop__   mow __boat__

seal __tweet__   pawn __flop__

Adverbs

Underline the adverbs in the sentences below. There might be more than one. Do you know which words they are describing?

She hit her head on the _very_ hard floor.

The sky was _extremely_ blue after the terrifying storm.

Traffic is moving _rather_ _quickly_ today.

The view from the mountaintop was _quite_ beautiful.

Lesson 153

Noun Basketball

Color the common nouns blue (colored) and the proper nouns red (untouched).

Lesson 155

Spelling

Write your spelling words on the lines below as they are read to you from the Parent's Guide. Learn from any spelling mistakes you make.

kitchen   staircase

instrument   ornament

shoreline   purchase

burden   surgeon

executive   judicial

legislative   jurisdiction

Lesson 156

Correct the Sentences

For each sentence, choose the sentence type by circling it. Then underline any words that need to be capitalized, and add any punctuation.

show your work on your math paper.

declarative — (imperative) — interrogative — exclamatory

Where can i find the spaghetti sauce(?)

declarative — imperative — (interrogative) — exclamatory

i'm so excited for my birthday!

declarative — imperative — interrogative — (exclamatory)

i like to go to epcot at disney world in florida

(declarative) — imperative — interrogative — exclamatory

Stop yelling at your sister(.)

declarative — (imperative) — interrogative — exclamatory

what is your favorite fruit(?)

declarative — imperative — (interrogative) — exclamatory

it's a very cloudy day today(.)

(declarative) — imperative — interrogative — exclamatory

I can't believe how hot it is today!

declarative — imperative — interrogative — (exclamatory)

Lesson 157

Homophones

Homophones are words that sound alike but have different spellings and/or meanings. For each sentence below, underline the homophone that best fits the sentence. Learn from any mistakes you make.

The ___ was eaten by the horse.	hay	hey
My backpack is ___.	knew	new
Rock climbing was quite the _____.	feet	feat
The bird _____ in the window.	flew	flu
My brother has _____ a lot this year.	groan	grown
I had to _____ the dough.	knead	need
It took us one _____ to get there.	our	hour

Homonyms

Homonyms are words that sound the same and have the same spelling but have different meanings. Read each sentence and fill in the homonym in the blanks.

the opposite of dark or the opposite of heavy _____ light

the side of a river or a place full of money _____ bank

to have fun or a form of theater _____ play

a tool with sharp teeth or past tense of see _____ saw

Lesson 166

Editing

Edit these sentences by underlining words that need to be capitalized and writing in any missing punctuation. Circle the words that are misspelled or misused. Do you know how to spell or use them properly?

sometimes when you got to the end of the year, it's easy to get a little brain dead. it's time for a scool break! You might be saying, i don't want to have to think anymore, but it's important to keep your brain focused and press on in your studys. Think about how much you've learned this year! You have written many different stories, essays, and main ideas. keep working hard in your writing. Maybe someday you'll have a published book on the market. If so, i would love to have read it!

We hope you had a great year with EP Language Arts 4.

EP provides free, complete, high quality online homeschool curriculum for children around the world. Find more of our courses and resources on our site, allinonehomeschool.com.

If you prefer offline materials, consider Genesis Curriculum which takes a book of the Bible and turns it into daily lessons in science, social studies, and language arts for your children to learn all together. The curriculum also includes learning Biblical languages. Genesis Curriculum offers Rainbow Readers and A Mind for Math, a math curriculum designed for about first through fourth grade to be done all together. Each math lesson is based on the day's Bible reading from the main curriculum. GC Steps is an offline preschool and kindergarten program. Learn more about our expanding curriculum on our site, GenesisCurriculum.com.

Made in the USA
Coppell, TX
04 August 2020